THE GLORIOUS
FIRST OF JUNE

1   Lord Howe
From the portrait by John Singleton Copley

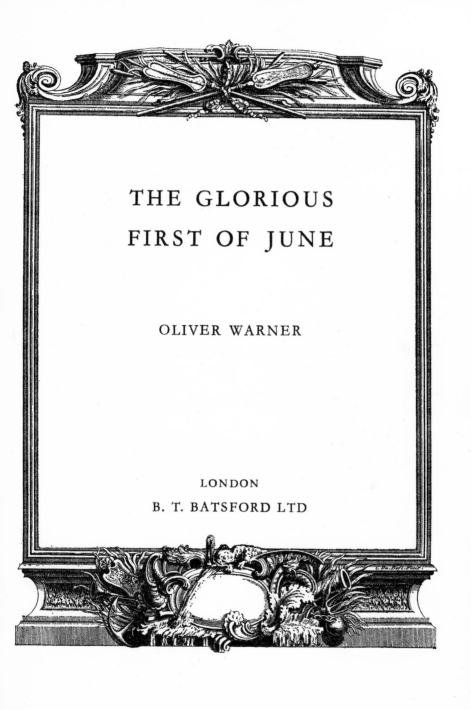

THE GLORIOUS
FIRST OF JUNE

OLIVER WARNER

LONDON
B. T. BATSFORD LTD

First published 1961

© OLIVER WARNER, 1961

MADE AND PRINTED IN GREAT BRITAIN BY
WILLIAM CLOWES AND SONS LTD, LONDON AND BECCLES
FOR THE PUBLISHERS
B. T. BATSFORD LTD
4 FITZHARDINGE STREET, PORTMAN SQUARE, LONDON W.I

To
R. A. L. Hartman

PREFACE

This study of Howe's battle of 1794, and of his methods on that occasion, is based on material, some of it hitherto unpublished, listed in a note following the narrative, where will be found acknowledgment of the discoveries of others working in the same field. Special thanks are due to Lord Bridport, and to the authorities of the National Maritime and the British Museums, for allowing facilities for the examination and use of manuscript material. The author is also grateful for the friendly help of Professor Michael Lewis, of Professor Christopher Lloyd of the Royal Naval College, Greenwich, and of Commander W. B. Rowbotham R.N. Mr. William Myson, Borough Librarian of Wimbledon, supplied an interesting reference, and his secretary, Mrs. Peters, cleverly read obscure handwriting and turned it into impeccable typescript.

Battle plans, based on those by Lieutenant Ballard serving in the *Queen*, reflect observations made from that ship, in each case simplified. The plans were published in *Logs of the Great Sea Fights*, edited in 1899 for the Navy Records Society, a learned body which has earned the blessing of all students of maritime history.

O.W.

Spring, 1961

CONTENTS

ACKNOWLEDGMENT

The Author and publishers wish to thank the following for permission to reproduce the illustrations which appear in this book:

Lord Bridport and the Trustees of the British Museum for fig. 29

Musée de la Marine for figs. 3, 12, 14, 18 and 25

The Director and Trustees of the National Maritime Museum for figs. 1, 6, 7, 17, 19, 21, 24, 26–28 and 34–36, and for figs. 16, 20, 31 and 33 from the Greenwich Hospital Collection

The National Portrait Gallery for figs. 15 and 22

The Parker Gallery for figs. 2, 23, 30 and 32

The Radio Times Hulton Picture Library for fig. 13

LIST OF ILLUSTRATIONS

I

Lord Howe

THE GLORIOUS FIRST OF JUNE, actually the climax of a
series of encounters, was fought in 1794—on a Sunday—between
the fleets of Lord Howe and Admiral Villaret-Joyeuse. It took
place in the North Atlantic, four hundred and twenty-nine miles
west of Ushant, farther out to sea than any other major action in
home waters of the days of sail. It was the first tactical victory of
the British in the war with Revolutionary and Napoleonic France
which lasted for over twenty years (1793–1815). Strategically, it
was not a success for Howe, since the French did what they most
wanted to do, which was to ensure the safe passage of a convoy
of grain from America to their needy country. That particular
outcome was not realised in England, at any rate by the public at
large, and the sight of six prizes at anchor at Spithead was a
tonic to a nation which had begun the war uncertainly, and whose
leaders saw no immediate prospect of any important success by
land. Its moral effect on the British fleet was lastingly good.

In his day, Lord Howe was known as taciturn—as unshakeable
as a rock, and as silent, Horace Walpole once said of him. As if to
emphasise the characteristic, little has been written about him
since his death, and some of that little is controversial. He left no
readily accessible mass of papers and documents, and such letters
as have been published are often as involved and stiff in expression
as they are beautiful in their hand-writing. Moreover an important
phrase which Nelson let fall about a "Lord Howe victory"—
meaning one which was not exploited to the limit—has been
remembered at Howe's expense.

While it is true that Howe represented the old navy and Nelson the new, that Howe relied upon tried methods and Nelson explored fresh ones, any idea that Nelson had anything but reverence for Howe can be dismissed at once, with proof to the contrary. When he held office as First Lord of the Admiralty, Howe gave Nelson his one and only peace-time command, the frigate *Boreas*, and Nelson was grateful. Later, Nelson achieved his own earlier successes as a flag officer under Lord St. Vincent, than whom Howe had no warmer admirer. ("Lord Howe wore blue breeches," St. Vincent was fond of saying, "and I love to follow his example even in my dress.") Finally, when news of the victory of the Nile reached London, Howe, who had long been at the head of his profession, and who later became the only man to have received the Order of the Garter for services purely naval in character, wrote at once to Nelson to add his congratulations to the shower he was then receiving.

Lord Howe's letter was addressed from Grafton Street on 3rd October 1798. It reached Nelson over three months later, when he was in Sicily, depressed that the Neapolitan land campaign he had advocated was in ruins, and overwhelmed with administrative work. Sweeping everything else on one side, he wrote:

> "It is only this moment that I had the invaluable approbation of the great, the immortal Earl Howe—an honour the most flattering a Sea-officer could receive, as it comes from the first and greatest Sea-officer the world has ever produced. . . ."

This was not entirely the language of hyperbole, and Nelson followed up his salute by describing the action he had won at Aboukir Bay in a few sentences of such clarity that they will always remain the best summary of the events of that fiery August night. He did so, he said, because it was to Howe that the Navy owed the efficiency of the system of signals then in use. He added:

> "I have never before, my Lord, detailed the Action to any one; but I should have thought it wrong to have kept it from one who is our great Master in Naval tactics and bravery. . . ."

The letter reached Howe during the last year of his life, and it must

16

have gratified him as coming from one who, though so many years his junior—Howe was commanding a ship of the line when Nelson was a baby—was obviously to succeed to the highest honours in their joint profession.

There is further detail to note about this incident, so creditable to both men. Sir Edward Berry, who had been Nelson's flag-captain at the Nile and was sent home with dispatches, met Lord Howe shortly after he had written his letter, and was able to tell Nelson that one of the things about the action which had most struck Howe was that "*every Captain* distinguished himself". This, said Howe, made the action "singular". In his own wide experience, he had not met with such a "band of brothers" as Nelson had managed to collect and train.

Time passed, and one day, nearly forty years after Howe's June action, King William IV was dining at the Brighton Pavilion with a group of naval friends. Among them was Sir Edward Codrington. He was an admiral of striking presence who had been captain of the *Orion* at Trafalgar and had commanded in chief at the Battle of Navarino in 1827, in the war of Greek liberation, the last full-scale fleet action fought wholly under sail. The talk turned upon Lord Howe: everyone agreed what a sad thing it was that no one had written his life. Codrington was specially disappointed that this was so, for he had known Howe well as a young man, and had served in his flagship at the Glorious First of June.

The King promised to do something about it, and shortly afterwards he summoned Sir John Barrow, Second Secretary of the Admiralty, requesting him to undertake the task. Barrow obeyed, though the task was not finished before William's reign was over. It remains to this day almost the only venture into Howe biography. Its imperfections are various, not all of them the fault of the author, and it was not, indeed, the shortcomings of Barrow which moved Sir Edward to put pen to paper so much as the impertinence of a reviewer. A gentleman writing in *The Spectator* in January 1838 actually attributed "shyness and want of nerve" to Lord Howe in his later years, when noticing

Barrow's book. This was too much. All who knew him, Horace Walpole—who did not like him—included, were never in doubt as to Howe's "constitutional intrepidity". Codrington, in angry justification of his revered master, made a series of notes about the man who had shown him the qualities of an admiral, and these he inter-leaved into his own copy of Barrow. Many years later Codrington's daughter, Lady Bourchier, included these notes, and many others, in a massive two-volume memoir of her father. Thanks to her daughterly affection, posterity has been enabled to follow the events of the sea campaign of June 1794 through the eyes of the young officer who was at the finest vantage point—the deck of Howe's *Queen Charlotte*—throughout the action.

William IV had suggested to Barrow that certain events in Howe's life would "require caution in touching upon". He did not, apparently, specify them in detail, but there is not much doubt that among them was Howe's failure to exploit his own victory. The idea that he had not done so was immediate, widespread in the fleet though not in the country at large, and justified. What blame can fairly be attached to him must be a matter for the reader's judgment, when he has considered the facts, and when he recalls Howe's age at the time of the battle. He was sixty-nine. He had himself once declared that no man over sixty should seek active responsibility at sea. If, as in his case, this was assumed at the personal request of a Sovereign to whom he was devoted, that was quite another thing. In such a matter, it would have been disloyal to refuse the burden.

Howe was, in fact, the oldest sea-officer to have won a naval victory on the scale of the First of June. His nearest rival was Adam Duncan, who beat the Dutch at Camperdown three years later, at the age of sixty-six. Rodney was sixty-four when he won the Battle of the Saints in 1782, and in the opinion of his brilliant second, Samuel Hood, failed as badly as Howe in following it up. Sir John Jervis, later the Earl of St. Vincent, was a year younger than Rodney when he beat the Spaniards, and of a toughness which preserved him till the age of eighty-eight. The future was with the younger men. Nelson was not quite forty when he de-

18

feated Brueys at the Nile, and Wellington much the same age when he began his unparalleled services in the Peninsula. A generous verdict would be that Howe's example was transformed by his young successors, but that none have exceeded him in the range of professional accomplishments, and in single-minded protracted devotion to the maritime affairs of his country.

"We can never really picture Nelson's fleet until we have understood Lord Howe's", wrote Archbishop David Mathew in *The Naval Heritage*. To understand Lord Howe is to appreciate not only the tradition upon which his successors built, but how much they improved upon it, a result due in equal parts to genius and to experience of prolonged warfare.

II

The French Republic declared war on Great Britain in February 1793, over a year before the battle. A state of belligerence could not long have been delayed, once the enemy had seized the Scheldt from Dutch control in violation of treaty obligations, and thus threatened British trade. For with a hostile sea-power based on Antwerp, North Sea traffic was in danger, and an important gateway to the Continent was barred.

Britain had been filled with horror at the execution of Louis XVI earlier in the year, and the decree of the French Convention offering "assistance to all people who wish to recover their liberty" was an act of provocation designed to create a fifth-column, as the phrase now is, in any country which preserved ancient forms of Government. The Jacobin extremists announced the intention of planting "50,000 Trees of Liberty in England", and there were some misguided enough to believe that it might be a good thing. Most of them soon learnt (from the bitter experience of other people) that a Tree of Liberty, planted by French hands on alien soil, meant a fight first against rapine and then against extinction.

The Prime Minister, William Pitt, was the son of the great Earl of Chatham, architect of victory in the Seven Years War (1756–1762) and a passionate denouncer of the conduct of the succeeding war of American Independence (1775–1783). It had been Pitt's hope and ambition, by means of increase of trade and conservative finance, to make his country strong again after her disaster and humiliation in the New World: to be as dynamic and successful in peace as his father had been in war. For a time, it seemed as if he would succeed. That he did not do so was the fault not of his own intention and leadership, but of events over which he could have no influence whatever.

These events had succeeded one another in rapid, almost bewildering succession: the formation of a French National Assembly in place of the ancient pattern of Three Estates, nobles, clergy and citizens; the storming of the Bastille, symbol of the old *régime*; the foiled attempt of the King to flee the country; declaration of war on Austria; the formal overthrow of the monarchy, finally the death of the King and the spread of a reign of terror, which was partly due to hysteria at the fact that foreign armies were at the frontiers of France.

Owing to a succession of alarms with both Spain and France in the years immediately before the opening of war, Britain was for once reasonably prepared by sea, and she had, moreover, a wealth of officers seasoned in two wars—some of them in three. Better still, she had in Howe and Hood men accustomed to manage large fleets, and it was to these admirals that the direction of affairs at sea was at first given. Hood, an autocratic character on the verge of seventy, but junior to Howe, under whom he had at one time served, was sent to the Mediterranean. Howe, who had always been an Atlantic man, was at the King's personal direction given chief command of what would now be called the Home Fleet and the Western Approaches. Each complained that the other had been given the pick of the resources: each in fact, was well equipped, by any earlier standard, for the beginning of a naval campaign. It has seldom been Britain's way to be *quite* ready for the next war.

Howe's earlier career is an illustration of what could be looked for in a senior commander, and he could be described as the epitome of the eighteenth century sea-officer. He had the advant-

2 *Commemoration Plate of the Victory of 1st June, with portraits of Admirals Howe, Graves, Bridport, Caldwell, Gardner, Pasley and Bowyer, and (below) of their captains*

By Bartolozzi, Landseer, Ryder and Stow, after R. Smirke, 1802

3   *The inner basin of the port of Brest*
    From the painting by J. F. Hue, 1794

age of social rank; he aspired to mastery of every side of naval activity; and he had had the luck to have been in vital areas in time of war. He had invariably emerged with credit, and not seldom with distinction.

On one side, his blood was German. His mother, Maria-Sophia-Charlotte von Kielmansegge, had come over as a child from Hanover with her mother, a favourite of George I. She had married into a landed family which had been prominent in the Revolution of 1688 and in the establishment of the Hanoverians after the death of Queen Anne. Howe, who was born in 1725, had been schooled at Westminster, that "fruitful nurserie" as Hakluyt had called it two centuries earlier. There he had come under the influence of a remarkable Headmaster, the enlightened John Nicholl whose pupils later included Gibbon, Warren Hastings, William Cowper, and Nelson's friend Sir William Hamilton. His education had been completed at sea, for at the age of fifteen he had sailed in the *Severn* on Anson's voyage of circumnavigation. His captain, Legge, had had to turn back owing to storm damage on reaching the South Atlantic, but his seamanship was of a high order, and Howe, in impressionable years, learnt much from him.

In the war with France and Spain which covered the years between 1739 and 1748, Howe had seen much service, and had been wounded in a frigate action off the coast of Scotland. This had been fought with French ships which were supporting the attempt of Prince Charles to recover the United Kingdom for the Stuarts.

At the beginning of the Seven Years War, Howe was a captain of established reputation. His capture of the French *Alcide* off the mouth of the St. Lawrence was one of the opening incidents. By the end of hostilities he had served as commodore in charge of the naval side of large-scale amphibious operations. Soon after succeeding his brother in the Irish peerage, he had led Hawke's line in the crack *Magnanime* at the victory of Quiberon Bay, which would have been a great moment in the most illustrious sea career. "I have tried my Lord Howe on most important occasions", said Hawke. "He never asked me how he was to execute any service entrusted to his charge, but always went straight forward, and performed it." He was, in fact, a "made man", and in the peace which followed he had served on the Board of Admiralty and in the political office of Treasurer of the Navy.

In 1775, as a vice-admiral, Howe had been commander-in-chief on the North American station in critical stages of the War of American Independence. He had conducted a series of skilful manœuvres in the face of a superior force under D'Estaing, the French having given their active help to the Colonists.

Howe resigned, on a serious difference with the Ministry then in office, and was in retirement some four years. He re-emerged to take command of the Channel Fleet, and in 1782, once again in the face of a greatly superior enemy, he relieved Gibraltar, which was then undergoing the final stages of its longest siege. To the end of his life he considered this his most difficult and successful achievement.

For five years (1783–1788) Howe was back at the Admiralty, this time as First Lord, and when he resigned office and was made an Earl in the English peerage, he might well have considered that his more active services were over, and that it would be only as an elder statesman that his voice would be heard. The dignities he held and valued, the ancient post of Vice-Admiral of England, and, later, the Generalship of Marines, were honorary. Having no further ambition, political or otherwise, he looked forward to the peace of a country life in the society of a devoted little family. But the King could not do without him. "Earl Richard", as he used to call him, was his favourite admiral, and in 1790 he was summoned to command the Channel Fleet once more, on a scare of war. That command was rarely relinquished for the remaining years of his life, though Howe was not, for some stretches of time, actually at sea, and at one stage was not even nominally in employment. But so long as he lived, he would be at the King's disposal when most needed. It was a case of tried devotion, for when George III had succeeded to the throne in 1760 Howe deliberated long, in his careful way, about his character, before making up his mind what to think of the young man who had been called upon to rule the country. One of his daughters once told Sir William Hotham:

> "... that her father was some time before he could like or understand the character of George III, but that, having done so, his Lordship formed a very exalted opinion of his Sovereign, and found him, upon any occasion, a man very much above courting popularity, highly honourable and dependable."

Howe, in giving his allegiance, was making sure of knowing precisely the sort of man he was serving. It was typical of his realism. No one is recorded as deceiving Lord Howe. He could be understanding, but he could not be fooled.

III

On 6 February 1793 Howe made an entry in his private journal stating that he:

> "Attended at St. James's to kiss the King's hand on my appointment by commission, dated the 1st of this month, to be admiral and Commander-in-Chief of the Fleet, for the time being employed, and to be employed, in Channel soundings. . . ."

The appointment was unusual in that it was uncommon—though not quite unprecedented—for a man who had held office as First Lord to serve at sea, where he would be under the control of a Board of Admiralty, the naval members of which would be his juniors. What made it more so was that Howe's successor in office was a man to whom he was "inimical". This was Pitt's elder brother, the second Earl of Chatham, who was to prove himself an indifferent naval administrator and an even less successful general. The family ability was concentrated in the younger brother, but even with the Prime Minister himself Howe did not always see eye to eye. He had in fact resigned office because he disagreed with Pitt's particular ideas of economy for the Navy, and because he was rigid in his refusal of personal favours. Pitt rarely asked anything for himself, but his friends were sometimes importunate, and Howe would do nothing for them except on the grounds of merit. Chatham was more amenable.

25

Howe's second-in-command in the Fleet was Vice-Admiral Graves, a man much the same age as his chief, with fighting experience in two wars. Next to him in seniority was Sir Alexander Hood, Lord Hood's younger brother, a man with whom Howe had little in common, and one who, in later years, treated his former chief with something less than the courtesy that Howe himself invariably showed. Howe's first captain, or chief of staff, was Sir Roger Curtis. This officer, upon whom the day to day running of the fleet depended, was in his forties, and for many years, ever since he had served as flag-captain at the time of the American War, he had been Howe's most assiduous pupil. The admiral relied on him much, and gave him his steadfast friendship.

On his record, Curtis should have been a good choice. He was at the height of his powers; he had experience in war; and he had proved his personal courage ashore, at the siege of Gibraltar, where Lord Heathfield had so depended on his exertions in the later stages that he called him his right hand. Curtis had been knighted for his success in repelling the attacks of Spanish floating batteries, and had been given a state pension of five hundred pounds a year. But, however intrepid on land, by sea Curtis was cautious. He was a careful manager, yet something of a fusser, with rooted prejudices, many of them stupid. There is not much doubt that Howe would have been better served by the flag- (or second-) captain who assumed command of the *Queen Charlotte* in 1794. This was the gallant and enterprising Sir Andrew Douglas, who was, however, considerably the junior of Curtis both in seniority and status.

The events of Howe's cruises of the summer of 1793 show the type of service he was at sea to carry out. They also illustrate the difficulty of bringing an enemy to action who had no intention of seeking full-scale encounter. Howe's instructions were "to protect the trade of the King's subjects", and to "molest the ships of war and trade of the enemy"—in other words, he was to combine cover for our own convoys with destruction of the enemy's. The duties were not often compatible, and if one or other employment had to be sacrificed, it was usually the second. There was also an intelligence report to the effect that French ships from Lorient and Rochefort might attempt to make Brest, in which case, a sortie against England or Ireland might be in prospect.

In the outcome, a French fleet of fifteen of the line was sighted on 1st August, but it evaded action. Another contact was made in November. It was rendered abortive through the fact that Captain Molloy in the *Caesar*, which was ahead of the other ships of the line, did not report what the look-out frigates had seen, and had duly passed on to him. The episode helped to convince Howe that his own ships were in poor condition, particularly as to their masts and rigging, that some of his captains lacked zeal and training, and that the French, when they wanted to, could show him a clean pair of heels. He was no believer in close blockade, a matter in which he differed from Hawke a generation before him, and from successors in the same command, such as St. Vincent and Cornwallis. Howe's idea was that the French ports should be watched by frigates or a detached squadron, but that the main fleet should lie ready in Torbay, cruising when reports came in that the enemy were active.

The channel fleet suffered so much from storm damage in the months between May and December 1793 that Howe was more than ever sure that his policy was right, but he incurred some odium through the fact that he had not been able to open the first year of war with a spectacular success. Some people even called him "Lord Torbay". Unpopularity did not affect him so long as it did not extend to the fleet—and it never did. He had known public disfavour before, and he despised opinion which was not based on sound principles. He would have reflected that Hawke had actually been burnt in effigy in London at the very time when he was pursuing Conflans among the rocks of Quiberon.

Landmen and seamen inhabited two separate worlds, and only the more informed landmen would realise that by his protection of the English trade in the summer of 1793, and by disrupting that of the enemy, which could be done by frigates and sloops, Howe was doing his duty. An encounter with the main

27

French fleet was only likely when the enemy was at sea in force in protection of a large convoy, or if he was covering troopships engaged in attempted invasion. Neither circumstance arose in the opening year of war. Howe could bide his time—he had, in fact, no other choice.

IV

By April 1794, weather damage from the previous year's sorties had been made good, and Howe's fleet was reassembled off St. Helens, Isle of Wight. There were thirty-two sail of the line, with attendant frigates. Howe would shortly need to detail some ships to protect outward convoys, and in particular that destined for the East Indies. These would be given close escort until they were in the latitude of Cape Finisterre and, therefore, beyond danger from a sortie from one of the French ports in the Bay of Biscay. Howe's admirals included, besides Graves and Sir Alexander Hood, Rear-Admirals Bowyer, Caldwell, Gardner, Pasley and Montagu, a galaxy reminiscent of the brave old days of Cromwell, Charles II and the wars with the Dutch. Montagu, the junior, was reserved for detached duty with the convoys.

The problems which confronted the French were the same in kind, but different in circumstance. Across the Atlantic, lying in the Chesapeake, were a hundred and seventeen ships, their holds filled with grain and stores for the relief of a country which, thanks to a bad harvest and political disturbance, was within measure of starvation. Any risk was worth running to get those vessels across the ocean, and great risks were taken. Their immediate main escort was to comprise four ships of the line under Admiral Vanstabel, who had reached America by the winter of 1793/4. Villaret-Joyeuse would sail the French fleet from Brest, provide the necessary cover from attack by the main fleet of the enemy, and there would be further support from a squadron under Rear-Admiral Neilly.

Howe's April cruise was uneventful. On 2nd May he sailed again from Spithead, having twenty-six ships of the line under his immediate command. He had detached six, ordering them to rejoin him with speed once the merchantmen were in safety. Two more ships of the line, not to be under his own command, would escort the Indiamen farther south.

By 5th May, Howe was off Ushant, where he learnt that his adversary had not yet sailed. The frigates *Latona* and *Phaeton*, supported by the *Orion*, made a reconnaissance and reported one ship of the line, with two frigates and two brigs, at anchor in Camaret Bay. Twenty-two larger ships, presumably of the line, were seen within the Goulet. Howe did not wish to prevent the French from putting to sea, since he was as eager to defeat them as to capture the convoy. He therefore made no attempt to watch the port, but advanced south-westerly, putting himself between the grain ships and their covering force, and in a position to deal with them first and fight Villaret-Joyeuse later.

A week passed, and Howe met nothing. Retracing his steps, he returned to Ushant, off which he arrived on 19th May. His frigates reported that Brest was empty, and brought the additional news, gathered from coastal shipping, that the French fleet—twenty-five of the line—had sailed three days before. Villaret-Joyeuse had been joined at sea by one more ship, and had actually passed close to Howe, unseen in the prevailing foggy weather.

After missing the French fleet, Howe's first move was to steer a course after Admiral Montagu and the convoys, but late at night on 21st May the *Queen Charlotte* nearly ran down a brig, the *Argo*, which was boarded.

> "We found her to be one of the Newfoundland ships coming home with fish", said Codrington, "which, with the convoy under the *Castor*, Captain Troubridge, had been taken by the French fleet. This occasioned the whole Fleet to be brought to; and after a consultation, arising out of the information given by some of the English crew still left on board the prize, a course was adopted for the French fleet instead of for Admiral Montagu's squadron."

One of the results of recapturing the brig (and some other vessels from the unlucky convoy), which had had only the protection of Troubridge's frigate, the *Castor*, was that Howe's fleet

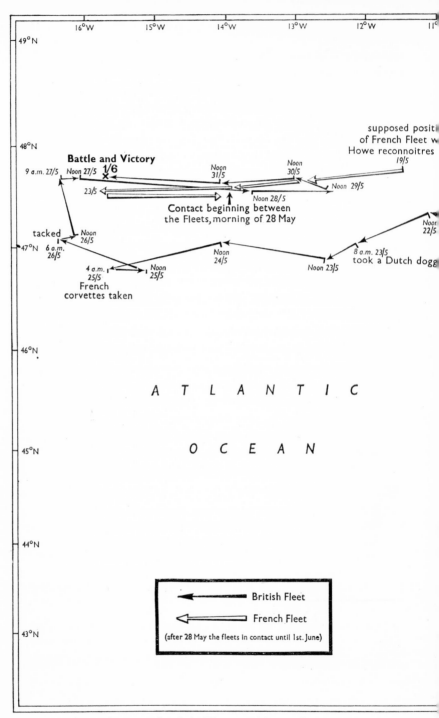

4 _Approximate tracks of the Fleets, 19 May—1 June, 1794_

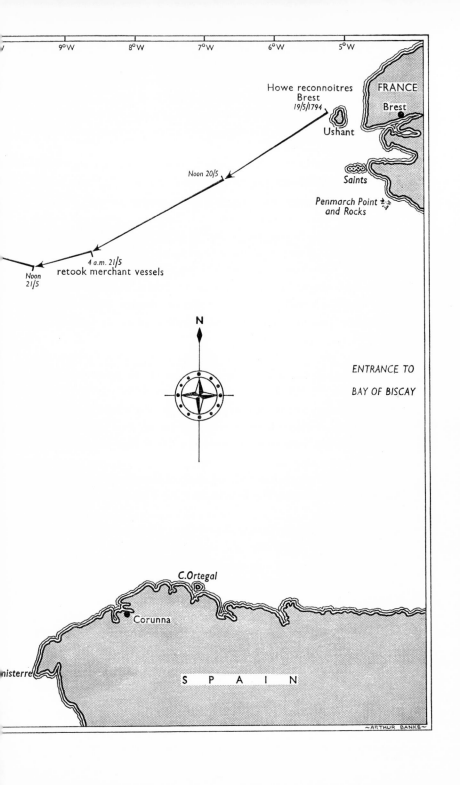

9°W   8°W   7°W   6°W   5°W

Howe reconnoitres
Brest
19/5/1794

FRANCE

Brest

Ushant

Noon 20/5

Saints

Penmarch Point
and Rocks

4 a.m. 21/5
retook merchant vessels

Noon
21/5

N

ENTRANCE TO

BAY OF BISCAY

C.Ortegal

Corunna

nisterre

S P A I N

~ARTHUR BANKS~

included a number of men from the French prize crews, all of them elated at their success, and all quite sure that, if and when the main forces met, they would be able to rejoin their friends. In point of fact, the *Castor* was recaptured by the *Carysfort* before she reached France.

On 25th May two corvettes out of Brest were sighted. They were steering after the British fleet, thinking it to be their own. Both were captured and burnt, Howe saying to his younger officers: "It must be very unpleasant for you gentlemen to see your promotions burnt: but I shall shortly be able to make you amends for it." Howe meant that, had he not destroyed the ships, they might have been taken into service as prizes, in charge of officers who would be likely to obtain a step in rank.

He destroyed these ships, and a few French merchantmen which were also met with, because, undermanned as he was, he could not spare prize crews.

Early on 28th May, with a rough sea running, frigates reported the enemy. Codrington, at the mast-head of the *Queen Charlotte*, soon saw the French ships to windward, about ten miles off. The relative position was important, since, with the advantage of the weather-gage, Villaret-Joyeuse could refuse action if he so wished, or attack in his own time. It was also likely that his force was between Howe and the French convoy.

At first, the French held on, but hauled their wind again when they saw that the size of the British fleet was a match for their own. Howe had formed his fastest sailing ships into a flying squadron, under Admiral Pasley in the *Bellerophon*. At 8.25 a.m. the *Queen Charlotte* hoisted signal No. 23, addressed to Pasley. This meant that the *Bellerophon* was "to reconnoitre or make discovery of the enemy or strange ships in view, and signify the same to the Admiral". It was an exciting moment, and Pasley being a diligent officer, he was soon not merely reconnoitring, but in action.

The French were distant, and it was not until nearly two o'clock that Howe made signal No. 35: "Take suitable stations for mutual support and engage the enemy as arriving up in succession." Five ships managed to get into action with the French rear, whose

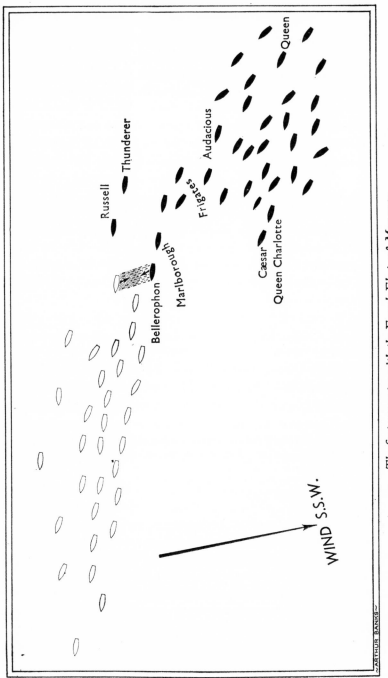

5 *The first encounter with the French Fleet, 28 May 1794*

(In this and subsequent diagrams, ships of the British Fleet are marked in black, those of the French Fleet in white)

~ARTHUR BANKS~

number included the three-decked *Révolutionnaire*. After a stiff fight with the *Russell, Bellerophon, Leviathan, Thunderer* and *Audacious*, she was so much mauled as to be unfit for further service. She was not secured, and, like the badly-damaged *Audacious*, she managed to reach a friendly port. The first round —since the *Révolutionnaire* was far larger than any of her opponents—was slightly in favour of the British, but by calling off the chase, and because of the lack of means to make any but the most elementary signals by night, Howe's advantage was not pushed home.

Next day, the 29th, Howe was still to leeward of the enemy, and his immediate object was to gain the weather gage. He determined if possible to break through the French line from his leeward position. The van failed in this object, thanks largely to wretched handling of the leading ship, the *Caesar*, Captain Molloy, but Howe himself, in the *Queen Charlotte*, together with two other ships, the *Bellerophon* and *Leviathan*, went through towards the rear of the enemy and cut off three Frenchmen.

As a result of her activity, the *Leviathan*, Captain Lord Hugh Seymour, was soon in trouble; her foremast was crippled and was in danger of falling. Howe instantly stood to her rescue.

> "On this occasion", wrote Seymour, "the gallant conduct of the *Queen Charlotte* in coming down to draw the enemy's fire from the *Leviathan* has made too strong an impression on my mind, and is too much the subject of general applause on board her for me to risk my sense of it, and offering, in the name of all the officers, as well as my own, this feeble though grateful tribute of our admiration of our noble chief Lord Howe."

The *Queen*, Admiral Gardner's flagship, also did well in the action, though her captain, Hutt, lost a leg, and did not long survive his wound. Howe commended the *Glory*, another three-decker, for her good gunnery.

In order to save his damaged ships, Villaret-Joyeuse bore down to their defence with most of his fleet. He saved them, though they, like the *Révolutionnaire*, were rendered unfit for further immediate fighting. The second round was decidedly with

Howe, for he had reduced the opposition, and Villaret-Joyeuse had lost the weather-gage. Howe could now attack, with his whole force, whenever he wished, provided the enemy stood his ground. If he did not, he could be chased across the broad ocean, and there would be stragglers in plenty for pursuers to snap up.

May 30th was foggy. Howe was content to keep in contact, while Villaret gradually edged away to leeward, slowly and skilfully enough to give his crippled ships a chance to get away, and for the convoy to gain distance. He was also lucky enough to be reinforced by five ships of Neilly's detached squadron, so that his strength was brought up again to at least what it was when he was first sighted.

At mid-day on 31st May the fog lifted, but Howe, with the moral strength which is the mark of a great commander, decided to postpone his final attack until next day, to make certain of the result. The actions of 28th and 29th May had taught him that some of his captains needed all the force of example. In the afternoon he was seen to smile, and the news spread like lightning round the flagship. "Black Dick", as they called him from his complexion, never smiled without reason.

On 1st June, hands were piped to breakfast. Howe then dressed his line with care, and ordered signal No. 34 from his *Signal Book for the Ships of War* which was then in general use in the Fleet, to be hoisted. This ran:

"... having the wind of the enemy, the Admiral means to pass between the ships in the line for engaging them to leeward."

The signal was not clearly understood throughout the fleet, and in some cases was considered to be permissive. Howe's intention was to bring on a *mêlée* by breaking through the enemy line at all points. His own prognostication was that he would take a prize for every British ship which obeyed his signal precisely—and he was exactly right. He noted the meritorious ships in his private journal: the *Queen Charlotte, Defence, Marlborough, Royal George, Queen* and *Brunswick*. In the fight which he brought about, six

Frenchmen were captured, while a seventh, the *Vengeur-du-Peuple* was sunk by gunfire—a rare event in the days of sail.

One hour after hoisting No. 34 Howe made another general signal, No. 36, to prevent any possibility of misunderstanding:

"Each ship independently to steer for and engage her opponent in the enemy's line."

One hour later still—at 9.30—the famous No. 5 was flown; this was: "To engage. If closer, a red pennant over the flag"—and Howe made sure that the red pennant was in evidence. By 12.25 the main action was over, and No. 102 was hoisted, which was for ships to close and join the Admiral forthwith.

By the time he had gained his victory, Howe was himself near exhaustion. He had won the final round triumphantly, and allowed the concluding stages to be ordered for him mainly by Sir Roger Curtis. Although it was a glorious day, it could have been more wonderful still if Howe had given rather more discretion to his subordinates in the matter of chasing or securing damaged ships, or if Curtis had not been so circumspect. But the squadrons were far from land: many ships were damaged, some seriously, in masts and spars; and what was certain beyond a peradventure was that the Fleet had secured a victory against an opponent strong in numbers and superior in guns.

Howe's conclusions, on viewing the scene of the engagement, were summarised in the official despatch which he composed next day from "*Queen Charlotte* at Sea . . . Ushant E ½ N, 140 leagues". They bear the impress of his individual and characteristic style:

"The greater number of the . . . ships of the British fleet were at this time so much disabled or widely separated, and under such circumstances with respect to those ships of the enemy in a state for action, and with which the firing was still continued, that two or three, even of their dismasted ships attempting to get away under a spritsail singly, or smaller sail raised on the stump of the foremast, could not be detained."

The homeward progress, untinctured with regrets of any kind, was recorded by Collingwood of the *Barfleur* as that of men who believed they had gained:

">... by the blessing and aid of God Almighty, as compleat a victory as ever was won upon the seas, more decided than we had just reason to expect, for the enemy was superior to us in strength and fought with a savage ferocity."

Collingwood later served in other battles and altered his views, but on 10th June, the day he wrote those words at sea, they would have been echoed by every companion-in-arms.

"We who were seamen were well acquainted with the great professional abilities of Lord Howe," Collingwood continued, "but he has outdone all opinion that could be formed. The proceedings of the 1st of June were like magic, and could only be effected by skill like his."

If such was the outline of the May–June encounters, reduced to its simplest terms, there soon came into being a mass of documentation, official and private, through which the background could be filled in. Dispatches were written: letters of proceedings were composed: copies of logs and journals were forwarded to London, and Collingwood was only one of many who wrote home. It is through such records, some made immediately and others recalled over the years, that posterity can apprehend in some detail the events of Howe's cruise.

2

The "Queen Charlotte"

WHEN Codrington first met Lord Howe he was a midshipman of twenty-three, looking forward to promotion to lieutenant, which for a man of his good connections and considerable service was overdue. He was friendly with the admiral's brother, General Sir William Howe, who, wishing to do the young man a favour, said to him one day in 1793: "Come here tomorrow morning. I want to take you to breakfast with my brother in Grafton Street."

When the meal was over, and the servants dismissed, Sir William said: "Now brother, I shall leave you together, for I know you want to talk." Codrington was slightly alarmed at this, because, as he said:

> ". . . there was a shyness and awkwardness in Lord Howe's manner which made him apparently difficult of approach, and gave him a character of austerity which did not really belong to him: but such was the fatherly kindness with which he spoke to me in talking over his proposal that I should serve in his flagship that, to my surprise, I found myself in a short time nearly as much at my ease with this man who was supposed to be so cold and morose, as I was with his brother."

Howe was married to a gentle and devoted wife, and had three much-loved daughters, one of whom, Lady Mary, was at Court, but it was a sadness that he had no son, and he found it good to open his heart to a young man to whom he had taken a fancy. He told Codrington how fortunate his brother Sir William seemed, with his easy manners and social grace, while he himself found it hard to get on with people.

Codrington was soon led into a discussion of his private affairs. He had been promised promotion by Lord Chatham, but, as the two peers were not friends, it seemed as if, in adhering to Lord Howe, Codrington might have to wait. "I suppose", said the admiral, "you would not like to go as midshipman in the ship where you afterwards are to be lieutenant?" "On the contrary, my Lord," said Codrington, "I should feel myself in a higher situation as mid in your flagship than in any other"—moreover, he would expect to be obeyed by the same men in either rank. The answer pleased Howe, and Codrington was soon off to join the *Queen Charlotte*.

Howe put the midshipman under the special care of the Master, James Bowen, who was a great character and much regarded. Bowen had given up a lucrative shore job to be with Howe, and, when Codrington first saw him, he:

> "had a pink umbrella, and was standing on the wharf looking at the ship when I was introduced. . . . He immediately said: 'What! are you the *youngster* I am to take care of. I expected to see a little boy, not a—fellow like you!' "

Howe employed Codrington in his cabin, drawing plans of the hold and matters of that sort, and he was told that he should do duty as "aide de camp". His promotion actually came through in May 1793, and then things happened swiftly. He was sent to the frigate *Pegasus*, Captain Barlow, so that he could learn to report the flagship's signals efficiently, before returning for duty in the *Queen Charlotte*. Sir Roger Curtis was jealous of Barlow, as being one of the admiral's favourites, and never gave him credit for what he did. Codrington, by working almost all round the clock, and by training two youngsters, brought the *Pegasus* to a state of perfection in her principal duty. So speedy became her men that one day, after Codrington had rejoined the flagship, they actually acknowledged a complicated signal as it was being run up by the *Charlotte's* halliards. "Damn that ship, how could she know what we meant?" said Curtis. Codrington, who was standing near, said: "Thank you, Sir Roger!"

By the time of the cruise of May 1794, Codrington was em-

6 *James Bowen, Master of the "Queen Charlotte", and later a Rear Admiral*
From a portrait by an unknown artist

7   *A sketch, made by Nicholas Pocock on board the frigate "Pegasus", "taken at ½ past 11 when Ld. Howe made the Signal to tack in succession from the van", in the opening phase of the action on 29th May, 1794. Hitherto unpublished*

ployed almost entirely on look-out duties, since he was long sighted, alert and active. He spent most of the daylight hours at the masthead, and, when he did go below, he used to fall asleep between mouthfuls of his dinner. The work being "harrassing and fatiguing", Howe had the kindly consideration to order him a chair on the quarterdeck.

II

Before the Atlantic engagements, Codrington was the recipient of some confidences of Lord Howe as to the manner in which he would prefer to engage. They were unique in their kind and they showed, in a striking way, Howe's uncertainty as to the quality of his officers. This was not as unusual as it may appear. Nelson had the chance, during the chase before the Nile, to create a unity among his captains remarkable in the days of sail, but it was Nelson who said that, *until* he had created that bond, "I would sooner have thought of flying than attacking the French in their position".

Howe said to Codrington that if he had his choice in engaging an enemy "with a good English fleet under him", he would like to do so by night, in spite of the difficulties of signalling. He gave as his reason that, at night, any superiority in discipline and seamanship would tell doubly, when opposed to a fleet of equal strength.

Just before Villaret-Joyeuse was met with, Codrington said: "I suppose, my Lord, from what you were saying lately, if we came up with the French fleet at night you will attack them at once?" Howe answered thoughtfully, "No," he said, "I require daylight to see how my captains will conduct themselves." This was an extraordinary confidence from an admiral to a junior officer.

From this remark, and from other evidence, the conclusion is warrantable that Howe not only felt that he could not rely implicitly on his captains' courage, but that he doubted their intelligence. "To *me*," said Rodney firmly, "to me belongs the painful duty of thinking." Howe would certainly have agreed with his predecessor in his view of what was the first prerogative of command. His admirals sometimes exercised initiative, and Howe was glad of it, but this was always within the strict framework of his tactical plans, which only the best of them seem to have grasped in their full complexity.

Translating thought into action with a fleet at sea must always present difficulties, due to unpredictable variations of weather and visibility, and the chance of damage to the flagship and to ships under command. An admiral's directions have, over the centuries, been conveyed in four distinct ways: (1) by verbal communication made before contact with the enemy, followed up by hailing when at sea or message by boat; (2) by written instructions, signalled by simple flag signals; (3) by more elaborate signalling, such as could be practised when, in the final decades of the eighteenth century, Kempenfelt and Howe had devised an efficient signal book; (4) by explanation of principles of attack and defence, wide discretion being left to captains as regards detail.

The first method belongs to the earlier days of naval warfare: the second to the Dutch wars of the seventeenth century and the opening wars of the eighteenth: the third was the method of Howe: the fourth was Nelson's, though it was seldom imitated by his succesors, who, by and large, have preferred a blend of the earlier systems.

Howe was such a precisionist that the story was put about that one of the captains at the Glorious First of June, wishing to find favour, gave so much attention to keeping his exact station in the line that he forgot to open fire. It was not true, but it made a valid point. Howe certainly never let any slackness escape his notice. He was justified in being strict. There were fine captains in his fleet. There were also others, though to read their journals and logs is to be left with the impression that they all did their best. It was the difference between one best and the next which was so extraordinary.

In the event, Howe's reservations were justified, especially in

the conduct of the *Caesar*, which moved him to repeated cen-
sure, expressed both by signal and in his private journal.

Captain Molloy had a brand-new ship of 80 guns, so fast that
she could outsail the rest of the fleet, and her appointed place was
in the van. But Molloy, who was a particular friend of Sir Roger
Curtis, had a ship's company who were restless under his discipline, and his idea of a fleet action was a distant cannonade. It
was a matter in which he differed radically not only from his chief,
but from the bolder of his fellow-captains, who, by and large,
did not like him.

When action was joined, Howe must have remembered many
unhappy incidents in the history of the Royal Navy, for, when one
of his officers let fall some disparaging remarks about the way in
which some of the ships were being handled, Howe said: "I
desire you to hold your tongue, Sir. I don't desire you to shut
your eyes, but I desire you to hold your tongue till I call upon you,
as I probably shall do hereafter, for your observations."

These remarks of the Admiral's reinforced others which he
had made privately to Codrington.

> "In case of going into battle", he said, "or in the conduct of
> any important event, make your observations freely as to your
> own opinion of the mode of proceedings of your superiors in
> command."

Codrington showed natural surprise, but qualifications followed.

> "I say it with reference to myself, for instance", continued
> Howe. "Make your remarks freely as to your own opinions of
> what is right or wrong, and even write them down—but take
> care to keep them to yourself. Refer to your remarks at a later
> period, and you will either, by that time, have found out the
> error of your own judgment, or will have had it confirmed by
> your own experience."

In the upshot, what struck Codrington most about his chief
was, in Lady Bourchier's words: "not his readiness to *engage* the
enemy, but his cool determination in *omitting* to do so on the
evening of 29th May, thereby running the risk of letting him
escape, in order to ensure the right conduct of the fleet". This was

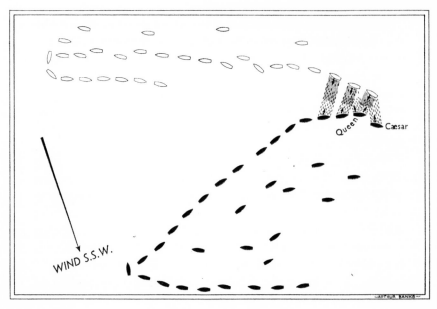

8   *29 May, 1794: the action begins*

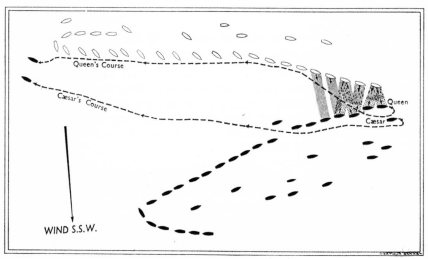

9   *29 May, 1794: the action develops: ships will follow the " Queen "*

in keeping with one of Codrington's own sayings, when in his turn he became a commander-in-chief:

> "I have observed throughout life that the test of a man's honour is money, and the test of his courage is responsibility."

III

Like every man who has ever stood in line of battle, Codrington was anxious about his own behaviour. How would he face the supreme test? His first taste of action was on 29th May, in the manœuvres which Howe made to cut off the rear of the French fleet, when he himself, together with the *Bellerophon* and *Leviathan*, cut through the line.

Codrington's battle post was on the lower deck, where the ports had been closed to prevent the sea washing in.

> "On going through the smoke", he said, "I hauled up a port, and could just see it was a French ship we were passing, and I successively hauled up the ports and myself fired the whole of my weather guns into her: then ran to leeward, and fired the lee guns into another ship. The weather guns bore first, as we went through on a slant, and therefore I had time for the lee guns. The breechings were mostly carried away, and guns running about: all the sand was washed away off the deck.
>
> "On going on deck, Bowen, in answer to my asking if I had done wrong in firing without any immediate order, said: 'I could have kissed you for it!' He added: 'In going through, the helm was hard up, and we were thinking we should not clear her, and we quite forgot to send you any orders.' "

Codrington's first taste of fighting had involved an act of initiative which had won him commendation and justified Howe's trust. It was also nearly his last, for he was flung from one side of the deck to the other by the recoil of a weather gun, on the second firing.

> "I found myself to leeward in the lee scuppers, in the water with which the deck was filled", he said. "I had no recollection how I got there. On leaning on my left arm I could just raise my hand out of the water. We were obliged to haul up the lee ports to let the water off the deck."

Royal George

Queen

WIND S.S.W.

ARTHUR BANKS

10   29 May, 1794: late stage of the action. The French have run down, and lost the weather-gage to Howe

The incident gives a graphic idea of weather conditions in the action. The *Queen Charlotte*'s log had an entry, the last of the day: "Most of the time we were in action the lower deck full of water and the pumps constantly at work."

Codrington recorded many incidents in the battle of 1st June. He had a cool head, and refused to let his men fire their guns until sure they would hit, though some of his fellow officers were not so particular. By this time, he had some reputation in the ship, so much so that:

> ". . . a man, the captain of a gun in Lieutenant Hale's quarters, asked me to fire his gun: and on my saying 'Oh no, nonsense'; he took me up in his arms and carried me, and putting me down at his gun, made me do so."

At one stage, Howe became convinced that the lower deck guns were firing into the *Invincible*, and he sent the first lieutenant down to say so. "*Invincible*," exclaimed Codrington, "why she is a French ship that has been firing at us all along!" "I know that," agreed the first lieutenant eagerly, "let's have a shot!" At that moment, Lord Howe came down to the deck in person and, thinking that it was Hale who had fired, struck him with his sword. Meanwhile Codrington's own guns were hard at it.

> "Just at this time," he wrote, "*Le Juste* fell off before the wind, and coming under our stern gave us two wicked shots in passing. Lord Howe saw her, as we did, with her colours up in the interval of firing . . . and was then convinced it was *not* the *Invincible*!"

One French shot went clean through seven feet of knee timbers, by Codrington's own measurement, and then struck a gun just in front of the charge, making such a dent that it could not be drawn. Another hit the muzzle of a main deck gun and split off a large piece, which killed or wounded ten men. One of them, a "little scrubby-looking fellow, whom he had not thought fit for much", was a pressed man. He showed splendid courage in action:

> "He was so badly wounded", said Codrington, "that Mr. Murray, the surgeon, seeing him, said: 'Why, what is the use of bringing

49

me down a poor fellow of this sort, why not let him die quietly, and not before the other wounded?' He had one eye knocked out, and both his hands shattered. He said nothing, and the surgeon had him put by, and went on with others. At last when the surgeon had several more brought down to the cockpit, he called out to him: 'I say, Mr. Surgeon, come, don't you mean to give me my turn?' He was then put to rights, and notwithstanding all his wounds recovered."

The most eminent of the *Queen Charlotte*'s casualties was the second captain, Sir Andrew Douglas. He was hit by a shot from the *Gibraltar*, which was still on the other side of the French fleet, since she had not broken through and made no attempt to do so. Douglas went below, had a bandage applied, and returned on deck, with the bandage in place of his hat. Sad to say, he had not long to live, and was ever afterwards in pain.

The action of the *Gibraltar* in firing at her own side, unavoidable on occasion, was due to pure inefficiency. This was specially remarked upon by Codrington to a lieutenant called Lloyd in the offending ship.

"Lloyd," said Codrington flatly, "how was it you were such cowards in the *Gibraltar*? The only ship you engaged was the *Queen Charlotte*." Lloyd's answer was: "You will be more surprised when I tell you we were not cowards, and this is the reason. Our captain, Mackenzie, is about the stupidest man possible. Having been signal midshipman with Lord Howe, I took the opportunity of saying : 'Captain Mackenzie, you have not been accustomed to signals. Will you allow me, as I have been signal midshipman in the *Queen Charlotte*, to go over the signals with you?' He said: 'I shall be very much obliged to you.' I dwelt particularly on the two signals: 'Each ship to take her opponent', and 'engage to leeward', which we had always understood Lord Howe would use. After the action, although those were the only two signals made before bearing down, Captain Mackenzie asked me if either of these two signals had ever been made."

It argues a great deal of stupidity, even in one who knew nothing of signalling, to fail to observe that his own broadside was aimed at the towering bulk of Howe's flagship.

IV

Codrington's observations of Lord Howe's personal conduct show how well he had taken to heart the advice of his admiral about keeping his eyes open. He saw nothing he could not admire. Three of his glimpses are valuable: Howe's conduct on 31st May; his anxieties towards the close of the action on 1st June; and his bodily weariness.

At daylight on 31st May, Curtis went in to Howe to make his report.

"I being an officer of the watch," said Codrington, "lifted up the canvas screen, by which alone the cabin (then cleared for action) was divided from the quarterdeck, for him to enter. Lord Howe was in his great coat, sitting in an arm chair, his only resting place from the time of our falling in with the enemy, and the following dialogue took place. 'Well, Sir, how is the weather?' 'My Lord, I am sorry to tell you that the fog is now so thick that we cannot see anything beyond our own ship', adding, 'and God knows whether we are standing into our own Fleet or that of the enemy.' I can never forget the contrast of Lord Howe's answer. 'Well, Sir, it can't be helped; we must wait with patience till the weather improves.' Instead of shyness or nervousness in these trying circumstances, Lord Howe evinced a heroic fortitude which may have been equalled, but never can have been exceeded.

"Upon the fog clearing up, about one o'clock in the afternoon, the French fleet were seen to leeward, showing every symptom of determination to sustain a battle. I watched Lord Howe's countenance when this report brought him to the quarterdeck to look at them: it expressed an animation of which, at his age, and after such fatigue of body and mind, I had not thought it capable: he seemed to contemplate the result as one of unbounded satisfaction.

"The Fleet were employed that evening in refitting and preparing for the impending battle. On the morning of the 1st June Lord Howe ordered the signals to be made for each ship to pass through the enemy's line and engage them from leeward, in order to make the battle decisive, and that each ship was to engage her proper opponent; and, addressing Sir Roger Curtis, he added, 'And now, Sir, prepare the signal for close action.' Sir Roger said, 'My lord, there is no signal for close action.' 'No, Sir, but there

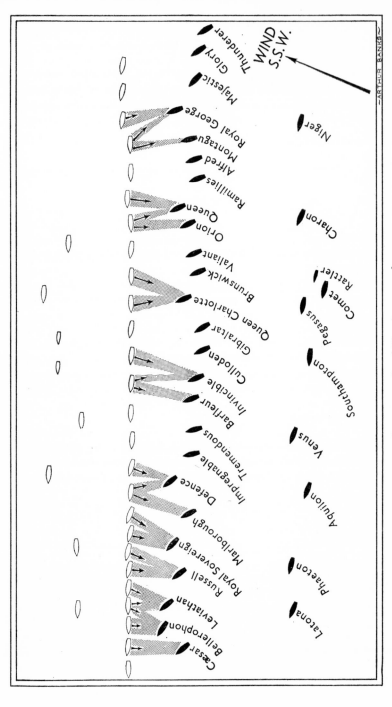

WIND
S.S.W.

~ARTHUR BANKS~

11   *1 June, 1794: Lord Howe's approach*

is a signal for *closer* action, and I only want that to be made in case of captains not doing their duty.' He then said, turning to us by whom he was surrounded, and shutting the little signal book he always carried about him, 'And now, gentlemen, no more book, no more signals. I look to you to do the duty of the *Queen Charlotte* in engaging the French admiral. I do not wish the ships to be bilge and bilge, but if you can lock the yardarms so much the better, the battle will be the sooner decided.' "

This surely is a passage in the conduct of war which deserves a place in remembrance. So does another, included in Barrow's life, which concerns the doughty Bowen.

"As the *Charlotte* was advancing down towards the French line," said Barrow, "with a determination to pass through it, it appeared so close and compact that Lord Howe expressed a doubt whether there was room to pass between the *Montagne* of 120 guns, and the *Jacobin* of 80, which had stretched partly under the lee of the former, as if afraid of the *Charlotte's* broadside . . . Lord Howe was determined to pass through, or run on board the enemy's flagship or the *Jacobin,* on which Bowen, with that blunt and resolute tone so peculiarly his own, called out 'That's right, *my lord,* the *Charlotte* will make room for herself!' "

Howe smiled, and officers around him recalled how he had once said to Bowen, "Pray, my good fellow, do give over that eternal my Lord, my Lord; don't you know I am called Black Dick in the fleet?"

Just as the *Queen Charlotte* was closing with the *Montagne,* Lord Howe, who was himself conning the ship, as he had the *Magnanime* among the rocks of Quiberon thirty-five years before, called out to Bowen to starboard the helm, Bowen remarked that if he did so they would be on board the *Jacobin.* "What is that to you, Sir," said Howe sharply. Bowen, a little nettled, then said in an under-tone, "Damn my eyes if *I* care if *you* don't: I'll go near enough to singe some of our whiskers!" The admiral heard him, and, turning to Sir Roger Curtis, said, "That's a fine fellow . . ."

Towards the close of the action, Codrington came upon the quarterdeck to find Bowen looking sulky. "What's the matter with you, old fellow?" he asked. "The Captain of the Fleet won't let us pursue the enemy", said Bowen.

"I then went on the poop to see Lord Howe," wrote Codrington, "who was looking anxiously over the taffrail waiting for the smoke to clear away and to decide what was next to be done. He had made the signal for all ships able to close round the Admiral, and seeing that the _Queen_, Gardner's ship, which had lost her mizenmast, was a considerable way down to leeward, and in danger of being cut off by the enemy . . . Lord Howe came to the fore part of the poop under great anxiety, and called eagerly to Sir R. Curtis, 'Go down to the _Queen_, Sir, go down to the _Queen_.' 'My Lord, we can't,' said Curtis, 'we're a mere wreck, the ship won't steer.' 'Then send everything else, Sir, directly.' 'My Lord, we're a mere wreck, and there are three sail of fresh ships coming down upon us. What can we do, when the ship herself won't steer?'

"Bowen then burst out with 'She _will_ steer, my Lord.' 'Try her, Sir', said Howe. And Bowen, with a seaman's eye, watching the movement of her falling off, and getting the spritsail well filled to assist her, got her before the wind with her head towards the enemy."

It was soon afterwards that Lord Howe at last went to bed, completely done up after the action.

"On such occasions", said Codrington, "one is enabled familiarly to approach a man in his situation. We all got round Lord Howe, indeed, I saved him from a tumble: he was so weak that from a roll of the ship he was nearly falling into the waist. 'Why, you hold me as if I were a child', he said good-humouredly."

One more scene in the flagship is related by Barrow, and shows the feeling of the lower deck for their Admiral.

"After the battle, a deputation of the petty officers and seamen requested Bowen to ask Lord Howe if they might have the gratification of congratulating his lordship on the victory he had gained, and of thanking him for having led them so gloriously. . . .

"On receiving them on the quarter-deck, Lord Howe was so affected that he could only say, with a faltering voice, and his eyes glistening with tears: 'No, no, I thank _you_—it is _you_ my brave lads—it is you, not I, that have conquered.' The honest and blunt Bowen, in telling this to a friend, said: 'I could myself have cried most heartily to see the veteran hero so affected.'"

3

The Enemy

LORD HOWE was not alone in having given a younger officer a glimpse into his aims and methods. It was so with his opponent, Louis-Thomas Villaret-Joyeuse. At the First of June the French Admiral suffered from a handicap that no commanding officer in English history has yet had to endure. He was subject to the advice and collaboration of a politician of a kind which later generations have learnt to call a Revolutionary Commissar. His name was Jean-Bon Saint-André, and his effect on the battle could have been dire. Thanks to the admiral's own qualities, the harm that Saint-André did was confined to a wordy and mendacious report on the behaviour of the professional seamen.

Villaret-Joyeuse was a Gascon, of gentle birth. He had originally been in the King's Guard: but the misfortune of killing an opponent in a duel caused him to transfer to the navy. He had done well, though in a closed society such as the navy of the Bourbons, he had lacked the interest necessary for promotion. He had commanded a fireship on active service in his early twenties, but he had stuck in the rank of *lieutenant de vaisseau*, and it seemed unlikely that, failing a miracle, he would ever rise higher.

The miracle occurred, and it was political. The ancient hierarchy crumbled and disappeared. Suddenly, under the giddy regimen of the Revolution, and at the age of forty-four, Villaret-Joyeuse had been made a rear-admiral. It was, in fact, a sensible appointment, perhaps the best in the circumstances, but it owed everything to the fact that the structure of the older French marine was undermined.

Villaret-Joyeuse never looked back, though he seldom en-
joyed anything but defensive successes. When, in due time,
Napoleon took power, he made Villaret-Joyeuse Governor of
Martinique, France's most important West Indian possession.
This island was lost to the British in 1809, but the admiral re-
mained in favour, and he died three years later as Governor of
Venice, a city which France then controlled.

It was on his way home from Martinique, as a prisoner of war,
that Villaret-Joyeuse disclosed something of his mind. He was
given passage in the *Belleisle*, a 74-gun ship, once the French
Formidable, which had been captured in 1795 from his own fleet,
and which had later served with distinction at Trafalgar. Her
captain was Edward Brenton, who at the time of the 1794 sea
campaign had been a midshipman.

Brenton described Villaret-Joyeuse as:

> "... a gentleman of high polish, and one of the best officers
> Suffren had in his fleet in the East Indies. He was a man of talent
> and bravery."

As a pupil of Pierre-André Suffren, a paragon who had died
twenty years earlier, Villaret-Joyeuse had been educated under
the eye of an admiral who was considered by the British to be the
best and most determined tactician they had ever fought.

Villaret-Joyeuse told Brenton that it was on the direct orders
of Robespierre, then at the height of his power, that he had taken
his fleet to sea:

> "... and, at his peril not to allow the great convoy to fall into
> the hands of Lord Howe. If he did so, his head should answer
> for it under the guillotine."

It was the paramount consideration of the convoy which ac-
counted for the delaying tactics adopted by the French fleet.
Villaret-Joyeuse added that:

> "... he only gave battle when he knew that the convoy was near
> at hand, and that it would fall a prey to the British fleet unless
> that fleet was disabled by action, or busied in securing prizes:
> for he had made up his mind to the loss of a few ships: 'What

did I care', he said, 'for half a dozen rotten old hulks which you took?' "

The captains of some of the ships which were made prizes would not have been flattered by their admiral's description, but his point was valid. Villaret-Joyeuse added that, while Howe had "amused himself refitting his captures", he himself had "saved his convoy—and his head".

Brenton, who had long intended to write a naval history whenever his career enabled him to do so, had the good sense to note the Frenchmen's words, and he traced with him, step by step, the twists and turns of the Atlantic sorties. The events were vivid in the memories of both men, since Brenton had been with Rear-Admiral Montagu's detached squadron. He had thus missed the battle, a fact about which he had strong feelings. Every word which Villaret-Joyeuse said served to reinforce them.

II

A citizen army can be created quickly. France proved it when no less than six thousand of her military officers emigrated, for political reasons, at the time of the Revolution. Twice at least, during the present century, the fact has been demonstrated anew. It is less easy to man and equip a navy almost from scratch, which was what had to be done when France made war in 1793. A fleet, even in the simpler days of sail, was essentially a technical armament. It required direction and co-ordination; accurate navigation; skill and man-power in the management of sails; skill and man-power to make a series of mobile batteries effective in battle. The politicians who guided affairs in Paris believed these proven truths to be nonsense. They affirmed that zeal could replace skill; that ardour could make up for lack of experience; that resolution could surmount lack of equipment; that the force of an idea—a country re-born, with living principles—could make up for deficiency in *matériel*.

It is a measure of the explosive force behind the Revolution that Frenchmen almost made their ideas for a fleet seem true. Although they failed, throughout the whole of the Revolutionary and Napoleonic war, to create a dominant sea power, yet they showed so creditably against what was, despite imperfections, the best-ordered maritime service known to the world—one with a tradition of what Mahan called "combat supremacy" stretching back to the Armada—that the wonder is that they did so much so well. Although he believed himself to be worth three of him, the British tarpaulin always retained his respect for the opponent he knew, irreverently, as "Johnny Crapeau".

Ironically, the French navy had seldom been more efficient than in the War of American Independence, the last which it fought before it became disintegrated. It had numerical strength, sound organisation, and varied experience, all essential ingredients in a service cast for a major role in a world campaign. Its ships were the admiration of British yards, as indeed they continued to be even when the men who worked them deteriorated. Four out of the five battle honours accredited to the Royal Navy which occur immediately before the war of 1793 were in respect of actions in the Far East fought against Suffren. Though inconclusive, they were as stubborn engagements as were ever fought.

By 1791, all had changed. There had been chronic and continuous insubordination in ships and dockyards alike. A return made in July of that year showed that three-quarters of the old corps of naval officers had disappeared:

> "Those familiar with the feelings of the officers," wrote Mahan, "will attribute them to the utter subversion of discipline, destructive to professional pride and personal self-respect . . . for which the weakness and military ignorance of the Constituent Assembly are mainly responsible."

Less than two years later, Grimouard, Philippe d'Orléans, Kersaint and D'Estaing, distinguished names in French naval annals, died on the scaffold. It was merciful that such men as Suffren, De Grasse, D'Orvilliers and La Motte-Piquet had been gathered to their fathers before they saw the ruin of pupils and comrades in arms. The survivors, when war came again, were

12 Rear Admiral François-Joseph
    Bouvet, second-in-command

*From a contemporary lithographic
        portrait*

13 *Admiral Villaret-Joyeuse,
      commander-in-chief*

*From the engraving by Forestier
after a portrait by Ambroise
            Tardieu*

14 *Jean-Bon Saint-André*
From the portrait by Jacques Louis David, 1795

blithely told by Jean-Bon Saint-André: "You will conquer . . . yes, you will conquer these eternal enemies of our nation. . . . You have but to will it, and it is done." How right was Captain Edouard Chevalier, in his history of the French marine, when he wrote that it is in the realm of *ideas* that one should look for the true explanation of those defects at sea which succeeded one another in the years of the war with Great Britain.

Ardour and patriotism were the thing—and in order to make sure that necessary zeal was generated, Jean-Bon Saint-André forced a decree through the National Convocation, which declared that:

> " . . . the captain and officers of any ship of the line belonging to the Republic who should haul down the National Colours to the ships, however numerous, of an enemy, unless the French ship should be so shattered as to be in danger of sinking before the crew could be saved, should be pronounced traitors to their country, and suffer death: and that the captain and officers of any frigate, corvette or smaller vessel, who should surrender to a force double their own, unless their ship was reduced to the before-mentioned extremity, should be punished in the same manner."

It is against the background of these words that some of the more extraordinary French accounts of naval actions should be considered. French naval officers needed to become adept at "justifications", though it was an insult to their bravery and intelligence that these should ever have been required.

As if to ensure that ardour should be given every possible handicap, Saint-André's next disservice to the French navy was to see that the old-established divisions of trained seamen gunners were disbanded. The Commissioner argued that these men formed an "aristocracy of artillerymen", whereas, according to his principles, no *exclusive* privileges of service, at sea or elsewhere, should ever be permitted. He took no notice of the words of Admiral Kerguelen, who pointed out that special training was needed to serve guns in ships. "Those on shore", he said (stressing the obvious because no politician seemed to be aware of it), "stand on a steady platform and fire at fixed objects; those at sea, on the contrary, are on a moving platform, and fire always on the move. . . ."

Throughout his administration of the navy, Saint-André showed a lack of practical sense which would have been amazing had it not been so typical of the doctrinaire mentality. The son of a fuller, at the time when he assumed direction of sea affairs, Saint André was over forty years of age. Seeing that as a youth he had been on one or two mercantile voyages, it might have been expected that he would have learnt the barest outline of realities afloat: but one of his earlier professions had been that of a minister of religion, and it was words, not practicalities, by which he lived. He became drunk with the ideas of patriotic zeal, attack and blind courage in action.

> "Disdaining skilful evolution," he wrote (concerning the infinitely complex art of naval warfare), "perhaps our seamen will think it more fitting and useful to try those boarding actions in which the Frenchman was always a conqueror, and thus astonish Europe with new prodigies of valour."

Sillier words were never pronounced by an intelligent man. Apart from the nonsense of supposing that Frenchmen always won at close quarters, how could even Frenchmen board, if they did not contrive, by "skilful evolution", to bring their ships alongside a (presumably) unwilling enemy? How right was Burke when he said of the Revolution which he so detested: "It is not a new power of an old kind. It is a new power of a new species." It proved to be formidable, but not, happily for Britain, in affairs of the navy. The new species was a land animal.

Villaret-Joyeuse himself would have agreed. The politicians, so he wrote, never remembered that "a man often is in a ship just as a bale is"—sheer lumber.

> "It must be frankly said," he continued, "it is not always the man at once most skilful and patriotic who has the suffrages of the political societies, but often the most intriguing and the falsest—he who, by effrontery and talk, has been able to impose on the majority."

Effrontery, talk and reorganisation resulted in Villaret-Joyeuse's fleet going into action for the first time with three flag-officers, two of whom, himself included, had recently been lieutenants, and the third a sub-lieutenant. Of the captains, three had been lieutenants, eleven sub-lieutenants, nine captains or mates of merchant-ships, one a boatswain, one a seaman. What the remaining captain was, before his elevation, is unknown to history.

As for the ships' companies, from the six ships which Howe captured, it was simple to calculate the high proportion of landmen to seamen in the French fleet. There was also much disease, some of it contagious, which Dr. Thomas Trotter, Physician of the British Fleet, attributed to the shockingly dirty state in which the French ships were found to be. The French sailor never cared for spit-and-polish: food was another matter. All ships were well stocked with sheep, goats and poultry. These, as Trotter pointed out, would have been consumed, in an English ship, solely by officers, or (through the officers' bounty) by the sick and wounded.

II

For all its deficiencies, so grave and glaring, brains were employed in the earlier strategical dispositions of the Revolutionary Navy. This was shown by the co-ordination of training and movement which was designed to ensure the safe passage of the grain convoy from America. A successful crossing was as important an issue as any which, at the time, faced the politicians in Paris. From the wreckage of the royalist navy they contrived to salvage enough ships and leaders capable of carrying through a major operation. If they were aided by fog and good fortune, the dispositions were sound enough in themselves to deserve blessing.

First went orders for French West Indies shipping to proceed south to the Chesapeake, under such protection as local forces could provide, the authorities in Paris having been assured of American sympathy, though not of military help. There they joined the grain ships. Then, in December 1793, Admiral Pierre-Jean Vanstabel, one of the few senior officers of the old navy remaining in the service of the Republic, was ordered to America with two 74-gun ships, *Le Jean Bart* and *Le Tigre*, together with lighter vessels, to provide escort for the merchantmen. Two more 74's joined him from France as soon as they were ready, and by February 1794 the armada was assembled. It sailed eastward on 11th April 1794.

On 6th May, Rear Admiral Joseph-Marie Neilly sailed from Rochefort with *Le Sans Pareil*, in which he flew his flag, in company with *L'Audacieux*, *Le Patriote*, *Le Téméraire* and *Le Trajan*, and a number of frigates and corvettes. Neilly's orders were to meet Vanstabel and to see him safely home. Villaret-Joyeuse's orders were to act as cover to the whole operation, and to face the British, if necessary, should they appear in strength. Three days after he had sailed from Brest, Villaret-Joyeuse was joined by *Le Patriote* from Neilly's squadron with the news that H.M.S. *Castor* and most of her convoy had been captured. Soon afterwards Villaret-Joyeuse himself had the satisfaction of taking a large proportion of a Dutch convoy bound for Lisbon. It seemed indeed as if the likelihood was that the French might have un-expected success in commerce destruction, without the necessity for a fleet action. The Atlantic was wide. The British might be evaded. This was pleasing to M. Jean-Bon Saint-André, who at least had the courage of his convictions, and had accompanied Villaret-Joyeuse to sea. His purpose was partly to report on how the seamen managed their affairs, partly as joint commander. It was a case of heads I win, tails you lose. If the operations were successful, Saint-André would share the credit, taking the major part of it himself. If they were not, it would be due solely to nautical stupidity. From his point of view, it was a perfect arrangement. He could interfere as much as he liked.

While Villaret-Joyeuse and Howe, with their fleets, acted as general cover to their respective convoys, Rear-Admiral George Montagu was detailed for the role of close escort to British con-voys. When he had succeeded in his immediate purpose, it was hoped that he would intercept Vanstabel, his French opposite number. With six ships of the line, he, Montagu, would possess superior force. The British Admiralty knew at least something of French movements and intentions, and Montagu was ordered to cruise between Cape Ortegal and the latitude of Belle Île, until 20th May. The orders were faulty:

> "The width, over two hundred miles, of the belt of ocean to be covered by six ships with accompanying frigates," says Admiral Mahan, "taken in connection with the chances which night and fog might give the French convoy for passing unobserved, illustrates the comparative disadvantages of lying in wait at the supposed point of arrival, instead of at the known point of departure, for a body of vessels whose precise destination is in doubt."

When, on 19th May, the frigate *Venus* met Howe, as she came with messages from Montagu, she brought news that Montagu had already taken a small French man-of-war, the *Maire-Guiton*, belonging to Neilly's force, and had recaptured part of Troubridge's convoy. The *Venus* had word, gleaned from prisoners, that Neilly and Vanstabel intended to join forces. Montagu hoped to intercept Neilly before he made his rendezvous.

Two days later, on his way towards Montagu, whom he thought might be in danger, Howe learnt of the direction which Villaret-Joyeuse had taken, and he guessed, first, that Montagu was in no danger, and then that Villaret-Joyeuse was likely to act independently, and would not shrink from battle.

The encounter of 28th May not only proved Howe right, but it showed something of the indiscipline obtaining in the French fleet. Captain Vandongen, commanding *Le Révolutionnaire*, engaged the British flying squadron in defiance of orders. A bold man, he believed that a three-decked ship was the equal of more than one 74. The survival of *Le Révolutionnaire* proved it: but she lost four hundred men, as against a handful in Pasley's attacking squadron, and it was necessary for Villaret-Joyeuse to detail a 74 to see her safely home. She was conducted to Rochefort by *L'Audacieux*, which had joined Villaret-Joyeuse from Neilly's squadron. As the name was similar to that of the British ship with which Captain Vandongen had been last engaged, this added confusion to accounts of the engagement.

Actually *L'Audacieux* had been sighted and chased by the British fleet on 25th May, when separated from Neilly. She had been detached to capture the *Rambler*, an American ship bound from Falmouth to Philadelphia with forty pipes of wine, and when seen she had her prize in tow. She cast her off, and eluded her pursuers, and she was able to give Neilly up-to-date news of Howe's movement. Then she joined Villaret-Joyeuse.

It was thought in both British and French fleets that the *Thunderer* could have taken *Le Révolutionnaire* had Bertie, her captain, shown more decision. The journal of the *Thunderer*'s master, Mr. Jackson, states:

> "... hailed Captain Parker (of the British *Audacious*) and asked whether the Frenchman had struck. The answer was he did not know. We passed the *Audacious* and hailed the Frenchman, who answered in English that he had struck and would follow us during the night."

That was satisfactory so far as it went, but nothing more was done. As darkness fell, the *Thunderer* rejoined the rest of the British Fleet, and *Le Révolutionnaire* was left to her own devices. A boarding party and a towing hawser might have gained Howe a splendid prize, but the chance was missed. In the state of the weather, and in view of the general ignorance whether Villaret-Joyeuse would be likely to make strong efforts to rescue Vandongen, it would have needed an exceptional officer and complete understanding between the *Thunderer* and *Audacious* to have gained the fullest advantage from this first encounter.

Captain Bertie's own account of the incident was sent in a letter to Lord Howe:

> "I hailed Captain Parker of the *Audacious*", he said, "and asked if the French ship had struck, he told me no. I then begged him to let me get between them, which I did, and it being very dark I determined not to leave her striking to doubtful issue, but ran close alongside and told him in French and English that my guns were pointed into him, but I would not fire till I got his answer if he would strike or not to the British flag. His answer was, 'I

66

do strike. You may send your boat when you please, or I will follow you tonight.' He then hauled down his colours.

"I beg to observe I take no merit to myself in his striking, the *Audacious* having the just claim to it, but that your Lordship may ascertain his positive capture.

"Seeing the *Audacious* coming up, I thought it my duty to make sail after the Fleet instead of remaining by a beaten ship, and made all sail about a quarter past ten o'clock."

III

The actions of 28th and 29th May showed that the French ships would be fought with determination, but Villaret-Joyeuse was as unlucky in *Le Montagnard*, which led his line, as Howe was with the *Caesar*. She did not follow his intentions, and she disappeared after 29th May, together with one frigate, *La Seine*. Both ships later reached France.

Villaret-Joyeuse, though he lost the advantage of the wind, showed both resolution and skill in bearing down to the rescue of *Le Tyrannicide* and *L'Indomptable*, which had been cut off by Howe's fleet. That evening, he had a stroke of luck, the first of two. He was joined with Captain Honoré Ganteaume in *Le Trente-et-un-Mai* from St. Malo. Ganteaume's 74 was a smart unit and his name was one to remember. Bonaparte would have said that, with his advent, things could not go far wrong with Villaret-Joyeuse. The captain had a charmed life. He did credit-ably at the First of June, lived to survive the holocaust of des-truction at the Battle of the Nile, took Bonaparte back from Egypt to France and an Imperial destiny in the Venetian-built *Muiron*, and was one of Villaret-Joyeuse's successors in the command at Brest.

On 30th May, the rest of Neilly's squadron, *Le Sans-Pareil, Le Trajan* and *Le Téméraire*, joined the main fleet. Villaret-Joyeuse's strength was then made up to what it was before the encounter of the 29th May. The new ships were fresh, and Neilly trans-ferred his flag from the 80-gun *Sans-Pareil* to the three-decked *Républicain*. Although he had sent home the ships damaged on the

29th, Villaret-Joyeuse could still meet Howe on favourable terms, and could hope to deal him such a blow that he would not interfere with the convoy. He had twenty-six sail of the line, one more than Howe since the damage to the *Audacious*, and heavier guns. But as the junction between Neilly and Vanstabel had not been made, and as Admiral Montagu was still at large, Vanstabel would need all his luck to get to France with his merchantmen intact.

Howe's caution in not attacking the French on 31st May, owing to weather conditions, gave the French confidence. Captain Courand of *Le Sans-Pareil* told Troubridge, who with about fifty of the *Castor*'s ship's company was his prisoner, that he had no opinion of the British nerve. Troubridge, who knew much of Howe, and who had closely observed his signals and manœuvres, answered "wait and see". After breakfast next day, Courand's attitude began to change.

When Howe's fleet began its approach, the French were ranged in the following order, beginning at the west, or van side: *Le Trajan*, 74; *L'Éole*, 74; *L'América*, 74; *Le Téméraire*, 74; *Le Terrible*, 110, a three-decker wearing the flag of Rear-Admiral Bouvet; *L'Impétueux*, 74; *Le Mucius*, 74; *Le Tourville*, 74; *Le Gasparin*, 74; *La Convention*, 74; *Le Trente-et-un-Mai*, 74; *Le Tyrannicide*, 74; *Le Juste*, 80; *Le Montagne*, 120, the largest ship on either side, with Villaret-Joyeuse and Saint-André both aboard; *Le Jacobin*, 80; *L'Achille*, 74; *Le Vengeur-du-Peuple*, 74; *Le Patriote*, 74; *Le Northumberland*, 74; *L'Entreprenant*, 74; *Le Jemmapes*, 74; *Le Neptune*, 74; *Le Pelletier*, 74; *Le Républicain*, 110, with Neilly's flag; *Le Sans-Pareil*, 80; and *Le Scipion*. The frigate *La Tamise* (formerly a British ship, like *Le Northumberland*, both French and British keeping up the custom of retaining the original names of prizes when they were taken into the captor's service) acted as repeating ship to *Le Montagne*, and very efficiently she did her duty.

All accounts agree that it was the French van which first opened fire on 1st June, and this well before half-past nine. As the French were to leeward, it had the effect of concealing their ships, to some degree, with their own smoke. Distant as the fire was, it seems to have had some deterrent value; the *Caesar*, *Gibraltar*, *Culloden* and *Brunswick* were all ordered to make more sail.

In her thrust between *Le Montagne* and *Le Jacobin*, the *Queen Charlotte* had her fore topmast shot away by *Le Jacobin*, but instead of following up her advantage, *Le Jacobin*, under the effect of Howe's fire, dropped away to leeward, leaving *Le Montagne* unsupported. She in her turn having sustained the force of British broadsides for more than an hour, then also fell away, first to lead a sortie against the badly-damaged *Queen*, then to rally the French ships and to rescue those which had suffered most severely. Villaret-Joyeuse's vigour and skill certainly saved *Le Républicain*, *Le Mucius* (which had actually struck), *Le Scipion* and *Le Jemmapes*, all of which were in extremity. Saint-André, in his official report, was brutally severe in his remarks on the conduct of Captain Gassin of *Le Jacobin*. He blamed him for the early confusion which afflicted the French line, and he gave him no credit for damaging the *Queen Charlotte*, which was in fact the means of saving *Le Montagne*.

The French were well supplied with frigates and lighter vessels. This was useful to them, since they were able to tow damaged ships out of action, and the frigates seem to have been handled with greater skill than the ships of the line. Some ships—on both sides—escaped lightly. Saint-André noted severely that *Le Trajan*, for instance, had only three men killed, while *L'Éole*, *Le Tourville*, *Le Jacobin*, *Le Pelletier*, and *Le Téméraire* all came off well. This appeared to be a source of grievance rather than of congratulation.

In the three actions in which he had been engaged, those of the 28th and 29th May and 1st June, Villaret-Joyeuse had shown ability in manœuvring poorly-manned ships, and he had made the most of their gunfire. He had refused to abandon vessels in difficulty, and he had given a good example of how an admiral should behave, never at any time losing control of his squadrons, and this despite very heavy loss in the flagship, the captain included, which could well have affected his signalling.

With Saint-André, it was another story. Once at sea, and unable, owing to weather and the presence of the enemy, to use his eloquence in encouraging the efforts of compatriots, he had to be content with observation and description—and his remarks on captains were never charitable. When battle was actually joined, he disappeared. "*Ah! le coquin!*" Villaret-Joyeuse exclaimed to Captain Brenton. "The moment the *Queen Charlotte* attacked us, he went down below, and we didn't see him again the whole battle." So much for example.* It was given out in the French National Convention that Saint-André had been "wounded by a block falling on his arm". Indeed, the man's good fortune and ingenuity never failed him throughout a long life. He died in 1814, ennobled by Napoléon, the possessor of the Cross of the Legion of Honour. By that time he was in the diplomatic service.

IV

The final moves of the campaign were between the French and Admiral Montagu. Ordered to cruise until 20th May, Montagu had extended his search, and did not return to Plymouth Sound until the end of the month.

On 3rd June, when off the Lizard, the frigate *Pallas* spoke Captain Parker of the damaged *Audacious*, got news of the French, and passed it at once to Montagu. Parker thought that Villaret-Joyeuse had at least thirty ships of the line, and Montagu sent word to the Admiralty that he intended to work all night to get his ships ready for sea.

With the help of the port admiral, who busied himself collecting every available vessel, Montagu was soon re-equipped to try to intercept Villaret-Joyeuse before he reached home. He had

* The *Anti-Jacobin* came out with a satiric verse on this episode:

> *Poor Jean was a gallant Captain,*
> *In battles much delighting:*
> *He fled full soon*
> *At the First of June*
> *But he bade the rest keep fighting.*

eight 74-gun ships, the *Hector*, wearing his flag, the *Theseus*,
Bellona, Colossus, Alexander, Ganges, Minotaur, Arrogant and the
Ruby of 64 guns, together with the frigates *Pallas, Concord* and
Circe. He was off Ushant by 8th June. This could have been the
supreme moment of the campaign. Had Howe been in pursuit of
the French, with Montagu lying in wait to dispute their safe
return to port, Villaret-Joyeuse could scarcely have escaped
disaster, perhaps annihilation. It seemed so even to him.

> "When, on the morning of 9th June, I saw your squadron between
> me and the land," he told Brenton, "I was petrified. My ships
> were in a shocking state, the lower decks crowded with invalids
> and wounded. A fight was the very last thing we would have
> chosen."

He was spared the horror. Montagu had at first chased a small
inshore squadron into Brest. Scarcely had he done so than he saw
Villaret-Joyeuse's topsails. The French fleet appeared to be in
good order, while two of Montagu's own ships were excessively
slow. Villaret-Joyeuse never showed up better. With his least
damaged ships he made for Montagu, pursued him for a short
distance and then, fearing to be drawn to leeward of his port, in
his partly crippled state, gave over the pursuit. Montagu,
apparently forgetful that, even if he could do no serious damage to
Villaret-Joyeuse, he might yet intercept the French convoy, bore
up for Plymouth. There were two big "ifs". *If* Howe had pursued, Villaret-Joyeuse would have found himself between two
fires. *If* Montagu, driven off by the French fleet, had again sought
Vanstabel and his convoy, he would have found them, and should
have ensured the destruction of escort and convoy alike, such was
his force.

On 11th June, the last alarm over, the French fleet anchored in
Bertheaume Roads, outside Brest, and Montagu made his way
back to England, having achieved nothing by his sortie. Saint-
André hesitated to enter the home port, so uncertain was he of
how the fleet, with its crippled ships and its lost companions-in-
arms, would be received. But on the night of 12th June the crews
saw lights in the Raz de Sein, the southern passage by which

Brest is approached. They were those of the long-expected convoy.

Vanstabel, fearing to find a hostile fleet barring the normal entrance, had steered for the Penmarch, a rocky cluster thirty miles south of the port. Two days later, on 14th June, convoy and fleet entered Brest together—in triumph. All had come well for Saint-André. He would devote the next few months to pointing out deficiencies in the fleet in which he had served, and in creating a legend about the heroic crew of the sunken *Vengeur*, victim of the *Brunswick*'s fire.

> "Thus ended the cruise," said Mahan, "which was marked, indeed, by a great naval disaster, but which had ensured the object for which it was undertaken."

Writing to the father of a midshipman in one of Howe's ships after news of the Atlantic encounters had reached him, Sir John Jervis, who was then at Martinique, said:

> "That battle was the best fought on our side of any since the Dutch War (i.e. of Charles II's reign) and I am grieved to learn that the consequences were not so propitious as the resolution of the parties who were engaged most merited. I allude to the arrival of the convoy from Virginia, the safety of which will enable the French to hold out another campaign. Had they given me the force I was promised when I left England, not one of those ships would have got out of the Chesapeake. . . ."*

* I am indebted for this reference, in Phillimore's *Life of Admiral of the Fleet Sir William Parker* (1876) to Commander W. B. Rowbotham. The possible strategical relevance of Jervis's force in the West Indies has been overlooked by most experts on Howe's sortie, since, in the event, it played no part outside the Caribbean.

4

Midshipman in the "Defence"

THE majority of Howe's force was made up of third-rates, 74-gun ships of the line. These, except for the *Bellerophon*, flying Pasley's flag, were private ships. By common consent, none of the 74's did better service on 1st June than the thirty-year old *Defence*, Captain James Gambier, and it so happens that one of her midshipmen left as close a record of events as did Codrington in Howe's flagship. William Henry Dillon also rose in course of time to the list of admirals, though he was never lucky enough to hoist his flag at sea.

Dillon, who came of an Irish family, was only thirteen at the time of the Glorious First of June. Though young, he was certainly not the youngest person present*—a baby is said to have been born shortly before the action to a woman present in the *Tremendous*. The infant, incidentally, received the Naval General Service Medal, with a clasp for the action, at the mature age of 54, when at last it was issued.

Dillon had been four years at sea at the time of the Atlantic actions, including service under Sir Andrew Douglas, a captain he much respected, though he once saw him, in a fit of exasperation, break a speaking-trumpet over a dilatory seaman's head.

He had been brought up to speak French, and it so happened that some of the officers from the captured corvettes became his messmates. Dillon's glimpses of the enemy are all the more

* The date of Dillon's birth is conjectural, but the view of the editor of his *Narrative*, Professor Michael Lewis, is that it was 8th August 1780.

valuable since he could understand them. One of the French officers, so he related, was:

> ". . . a gentleman of fortune who had been ruined by the Revolution, and taken to the naval service of his country as his last resource. . . . He spoke in very high terms of the discipline of the French Fleet, making quite sure we should be beaten when we brought them to action. Nevertheless he could not help expressing his astonishment at the cleanliness and good order of the *Defence*, which led him at times to let slip remarks indicating apprehensions and doubts of the final success of his countrymen in the day of trial. He watched all the motions of the fleet with extreme anxiety, and the manœuvre which seemed to attract his attention most was the rapidity with which our ships were tacked, often within five minutes; whereas the French ships he told us, were always a $\frac{1}{4}$ of an hour under that evolution."

When Villaret-Joyeuse was sighted, all was elation: "no more sulky looks", said Dillon. Ships cheered one another. "Death or Victory was the prevailing feeling." Captain Gambier, a religious man known behind his back as "Preaching Jemmy", and a friend of members of the Clapham Sect such as William Wilberforce and Zachary Macaulay, was all activity. He "exerted himself in a wonderful manner", said his admiring midshipmen, "determined to set a noble example to all under his command".

The *Defence*, which was in Graves's division, took no part in the fighting on 28th May, but was engaged with a three-decker in the somewhat confused action of the following day, when Dillon first found himself under fire.

> "One or two shots passed so close to the Captain that I thought he was hit", said Dillon. "He clapped both hands upon his thighs with some emotion; then, recovering himself, he took out of his pocket a piece of biscuit, and began eating it as if nothing had happened. He had evidently been shook by the wind of a shot. He had on a cocked hat, and kept walking the deck, cheering up the seamen with the greatest coolness."

Dillon soon saw a man killed, blood and brains spattering the deck, with men around him wounded. Further shots made havoc on the poop, cutting away the main brace. "Some of the men could not help showing symptoms of alarm," said Dillon, "which the Captain noticing, he instantly went up, and, calling the seamen together, led them to set the brace to rights." Gambier had all the best ideas: coolness, example, activity in leadership.

The firing was distant, and when the *Defence*'s gunners found they could not reach the Frenchmen, even with their pieces at extreme elevation, they ceased fire. Presently, one of the British three-deckers, the *Glory*, Captain Elphinstone, closed in, drew the enemy's attention and received their shot.

II

The First of June was the *Defence*'s great day, but the breakfast for which Howe had so carefully given time was not much of a meal.

> "All the tables and conveniences were stowed below . . . nothing to be seen on the decks but powder, shot, ramrods and instruments of destruction. Whilst the ship's company were making the best of the time allowed for refreshment, the Captain collected most of his officers in the Cabin, where a short prayer suitable to the occasion was offered to the Almighty for protection against the impending events."

This incident was characteristic of Gambier, but it was not much enjoyed—for Gambier's religion was gloomier than his personal conduct. After prayers he went round the ship, and spoke to everyone in terms of encouragement. "The noblest feelings of patriotism were proclaimed", said Dillon: "a determination to conquer prevailed."

Gambier took the *Defence* down upon the enemy in bold fashion. She was the only ship in Howe's line to have her main topgallant sail set. "Look at the *Defence*", said the commander-in-chief when he saw her. "See how nobly she is going into action!" Actually, by carrying so much canvas, Gambier was exposing himself unnecessarily, since he would reach the enemy line in advance of others, and unsupported. When asked whether he would not reduce sail, he said: "I am acting in obedience to the Admiral's signal."

Shortly after 9 o'clock the French opened fire, and Dillon went to his quarters below. The *Defence* reserved her fire till she was close to the enemy, and Dillon heard the first shots strike a French hull. It was the custom in the *Defence*, and elsewhere, to lower the ports whilst loading the guns. This was an innovation which had been made possible by fitting the spoons, sponges, rammers and worms, the principal implements for serving the guns, with flexible staves, so that the men would not be exposed while reloading. In some of the French vessels men had to climb almost outside the ship to clean and reload their weapons, and it was a service for which, in face of British fire, there were no eager volunteers.

> "After the first two or three broadsides," said Dillon, "I became anxious to have a good view of the ship we were engaging. . . . I required the men at the foremost gun to allow me a few seconds, when the port was hauled up, to look out from it. . . . I beheld our antagonist firing away at us in quick succession; the ship was painted a dark red, as most of the fleet were, to denote their sanguinary feelings against their adversaries.
>
> "I had not enjoyed the sight long—only a few seconds—when a rolling sea came in and completely covered me. The tars, noticing this, instantly let down the port, but I got a regular soaking for my curiosity."

Dillon soon saw a casualty. It was a man called John Polly, who was so short that he remarked that shot would pass over him.

> "The words had not been long out of his mouth," said Dillon, "when a shot cut his head right in two, leaving the tip of each ear remaining on the lower part of the cheek. . . . The head of this unfortunate seaman was cut so horizontally, that anyone looking at it would have supposed it had been done by the blow of an axe. His body was committed to the deep."

Polly's remains were thrown overboard without ceremony. That was the fate of men killed in action.

At 10.30 the *Defence*'s mizenmast was shot away, and the ship began to drift to leeward. By that time, there had been other casualties in Dillon's group of guns. One man, Holmes, had lost an arm close to the shoulder, and as the guns on both sides of the

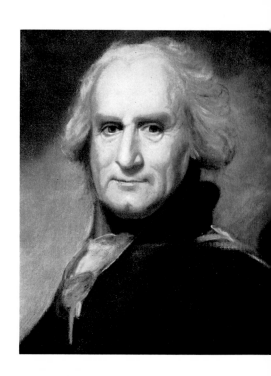

17 *Sir Alexander Hood, K.B.*

*From the portrait by
L. F. Abbott*

18 *Captain Renaudin,
of "Le Vengeur"*

*From a contemporary
bas-relief*

ship were being used, the strain on the crews was considerable. It was relieved in an unexpected way. At 11.30 the ship lost her mainmast, which fell with a terrific crash. The surviving men from the tops, main and mizen, were then ordered below to help serve the ordnance.

> "They reported the upper and the quarterdeck to be dreadfully shattered", said Dillon. "The lower deck was at times so completely filled with smoke that we could scarcely distinguish each other, and the guns were so heated that, when fired, they nearly kicked the upper deck beams. The metal became so hot that fearing some accident, we reduced the quantity of powder, allowing also more time to elapse between the loading and firing of them."

One of the gun captains was a Swede, serving under the name of John West. Dillon had noticed his backwardness, and, when the midshipman was engaged elsewhere, John Lee, the second captain of West's gun, came up to report that West had deserted his quarters. "Why didn't you knock him down?" said Dillon. "I did, Sir," said Lee promptly, "with this handspike." All the same, West had vanished, and by now everyone's energies were taken up with securing a gun which had broken loose and was causing harm and confusion.

One of the lieutenants thought he noticed signs of men failing to exert themselves, and drew his sword, threatening to lay about him.

> "The tars", said Dillon, "were rather astonished at this proceeding of their officer as, hitherto, he had approved of their conduct. They had been fighting upwards of two hours, and naturally were fatigued. They explained their anxiety to do their best. This pacified the heroic lieutenant. He sheathed his sword, and the men went on at the guns as before."

Dillon was soon afterwards blown backwards by the wind of a shot, falling senseless, jammed between two men. He was helped up, and friends began rubbing his limbs. He had a wound in his cheek, and was very thirsty, but the water he was given was salt. The two men who had fallen with him, so it then appeared, had both been killed by the wind of the shot.

When the action seemed almost over, orders came from the quarterdeck for all hands to lie down. An enemy three-decker was approaching, and as the *Defence* could not steer, her helm being lashed a-lee, it seemed likely that she would be raked, with dire effects. "This, to me, was the most awful part of the battle", said Dillon.

So also thought one of the lieutenants, whose station was at the after part of the main deck. Barrow, in his *Life of Howe*, says that he was:

> "... struck with a kind of momentary panic, and ran up to the quarterdeck, and addressing the captain with great eagerness exclaimed : 'Damn my eyes, Sir, but here is a whole mountain coming upon us: what shall we do?' Captain Gambier, unmoved, and looking gravely at him, said in a solemn tone: 'How dare you, Sir, at this awful moment, come to me with an oath in your mouth? Go down, Sir, and encourage your men to stand to their guns, like brave British seamen.'"

Barrow actually asked Gambier, some years after the battle, if the incident were true. Gambier drily said he believed something of the sort did happen.

Fortunately, the powerful Frenchman was not in much of a state to take advantage of his opportunity, and, in crossing the *Defence*'s stern, "to our astonishment", said Dillon, "he only fired a few random shot, which brought down our disabled foremast". As the Frenchman went by the enemy found, to their cost, that Gambier still had guns in action. They could hit.

> "In watching the motions of this ship," said Dillon, "I noticed that the Frenchmen, in many instances, loaded their guns from the outside. One man I distinctly saw riding upon a lower deck gun, loading it. He was stripped from the waist upwards, and had we been sufficiently near, our marines could have picked him off with their muskets."

By this time it was past mid-day, and the main battle was over.

> "My clothes were still damp," said Dillon, "my shoes, to which I had small buckles, were covered with blood, my face and hands smutched (*sic*) with powder and blood. At my quarters I had

14 men killed and wounded (if I included myself I should say 15); and a gun. I now ascertained that no part of the lower deck had suffered so much as mine. On my way aft I shook hands with other Mids who had escaped."

One of these midshipmen, Consitt, had been acting as Gambier's A.D.C. He left an account which supplements and confirms Dillon, including the fact that the *Royal Sovereign*, which went to the help of the *Defence*, at first mistook her for a Frenchman, and caused some casualties, including men of the Queen's Royal Regiment (2nd Foot) who were serving in the Fleet as marines. Consitt also remarked that "red ensigns were universally hoisted" by the British fleet. If this was so, it was possibly the last occasion in a general action. At Cape St. Vincent, the Nile and Trafalgar, the white ensign was flown, in order that there should be no confusion with Spanish and French flags.

Exploring quarterdeck and poop, Dillon came upon the Captain.

"He noticed me very kindly," said the midshipman, "and in replying to his questions I related what had happened at my quarters. While in conversation with him, the Second Lieutenant began firing some of the starboard maindeck guns. He was drunk. By this rash act he set the ship on fire, as the foretopsail was lying over the side. But in due time the fire was extinguished, and our alarms at an end."

III

Dillon's account of what happened after the battle, and in the days immediately following the return of the fleet to Spithead, is full enough to share in some detail, before returning to the Atlantic to observe incidents elsewhere. Although Dillon developed into a sententious, even pompous, character in later life, he had the sense to use his eyes and to keep notes, and he never lost that passionate interest in everything to do with his profession which he had had from the day when, as a mere child, his name was first entered on a ship's books.

The great necessity for the *Defence* was a tow. Gambier signalled for help from the stump of the mizen, and it soon came. Meanwhile:

> "... in clearing away the lumber on the poop, a marine was found stowed away under the hen coops. Those who lugged him out thought him dead. However, he soon came to life ... one of the finest limbed men I ever beheld, and the most perfect in his exercise. All hands laughed at him when they saw he had not been hurt. He was also," said Dillon in extenuation, "like my friend West, a foreigner."

Shortly after the battle, the *Queen Charlotte* passed near Dillon's ship. The *Defence* gave her "three hearty cheers". Howe was still on deck, and said: "If every ship of the fleet had followed Captain Gambier's example, the result of the action would have been very different from what it is." He never made a more just observation.

Dillon, looking round him, calculated that there were fourteen ships of the line largely dismasted, twelve of them Frenchmen. The *Defence* and the *Marlborough*, Captain Berkeley, were the only two British ships which had suffered equally.

> "Captain Gambier," said Dillon, "giving me his spy-glass (which had been hit by a shot) desired me to let him know the number of ships with topgallant yards across."

Dillon and a friend set to work, and made out eighteen in Howe's fleet, which meant that they were, in appearance at any rate, still fit to go into battle. Everyone in the *Defence* expected the fight to be renewed, and were astonished that there was no signal.

Captain Troubridge, lately of the *Castor*, who had been on board the *Sans-Pareil*, had been asked to haul down her colours. He was, says Dillon, "quite lost at Lord Howe's inactivity". So were many others. "Had the French been brought to action that afternoon," said Dillon with the wisdom of hind-sight, "the result would have been the most splendid victory ever achieved on the ocean."

While the men of the *Defence* were clearing up, the *Invincible*, Captain Pakenham, hailed them. "Jemmy," said Pakenham to his friend Gambier, "whom the Lord loveth He chasteneth!"

Gambier asked Pakenham how many he had lost. "Damn me if

I know", came the answer. "They won't tell me, for fear I should stop their grog." The living were, for the time being, enjoying the tots of their deceased shipmates.

The *Invincible* was an Irish ship, and Pakenham presently sent an officer over to Gambier.

> "I shall never forget that gentleman", said Dillon. "When he came alongside he was dressed in a guernsey jacket with a welch wig, and had not the slightest appearance of an officer, as all the boat's crew were similarly attired.
>
> "When he reached the quarterdeck, we ascertained by the buttons of his smalls that he was a Lieutenant—McGuire. He was presented to the Captain, to whom he had been sent to offer us assistance. Captain Gambier naturally put many questions to him relating to the action. His replies were delivered with many oaths, which so disgusted our chief that he turned his back and left him. The Lieutenant then, very quietly folding his arms, seated himself on the stump of the mainmast, but as none of the *Defence*'s seemed inclined to take further notice of him after his rudeness, he left the ship."

Poor McGuire. It is improbable that his rough language to a superior officer was intentional. Captain Pakenham, perhaps deliberately, seems not to have warned him of the sort of man he had been sent to see.

Next came the frigate *Phaeton*, Captain William Bentinck, with orders to take the *Defence* in tow. As she did so, the *Valiant* came alongside, her captain, Pringle (who had done well himself), paying many compliments to Gambier, saying that he had sunk an enemy ship, *L'Éole*. It was not so, though there was a general belief to that effect in Howe's fleet.

Dillon soon went below, to see how his wounded men were getting on. Lee was full of spirits, and when Dillon told him how the day had gone, he said: "Then I don't mind the loss of my arm. I am satisfied." So was another gunner, who had lost part of his, and:

> "... was quite cheerful, not seeming to mind his misfortune. He was eating a piece of buttered biscuit as if nothing had happened. It was a very gratifying circumstance to witness so many acts of heroic bravery that were displayed on board a

ship. Patriotic sentences were uttered that would have done honour to the noblest minds: yet these were expressed by the humblest class of men."

It was so in all ships, in days before Englishmen had learnt to suppress their feelings, or, as a cynic might say, before they had lost their innocence.

West, the absconding Swede, had told a good story. Dillon asked if he had been down for attention. "Yes," said the surgeon, "for a bruise on the neck." "That", said Dillon, "was a blow he received from the second captain of his gun with a handspike, for deserting his quarters." West had stayed snug for the rest of the battle.

The ship the *Defence* most admired was Gardner's flagship, the three-decked *Queen* which had fought superbly, though her captain, Hutt, had been so badly wounded that he did not long survive. Dillon wrote:

> ". . . she astonished us by her extraordinary exertions. . . . She had lost her mainmast. This was replaced in a most able manner before the evening . . . all her sides were scrubbed, her paint-work looking as clean as if nothing had happened—a good proof of what can be done with good discipline and management."

IV

There was fine weather after the action, and during the first night, while the ship was in tow of the *Phaeton*, all was well. The *Defence* continued putting things to rights. There were anxious moments about the tow itself, and no wonder, for the *Phaeton*'s Master recorded that at two o'clock on the day of the battle:

> ". . . the hawser broke and was lost all but 10 fathoms, and lost a deep sea line one hundred and fifty fathoms in length in lowering it over the stern into the boat. Sent an end of a cable on board the *Defence* and hauled on board the end of her stream cable. Made sail and stood to the westward."

Next morning, the frigate was relieved—to everyone's surprise—by the *Caesar*, whose captain, Molloy, was in such disfavour with the admiral.

"When he came on board the *Defence*," said Dillon, "he was anxious to argue the point with Captain Gambier, but our chief would not listen to a word. They soon parted. Our captain was conscious of having done his duty; therefore he determined not to meddle with the conduct of others. The *Defence* was the first ship of the British fleet that broke through the enemy's line. This gallant act was notorious, and the Captain deserved all the consideration due to the merits of the case."

The joke in the fleet was that the *Defence* had not been at prayers *that* morning.

On the afternoon of the 2nd, the French fleet was sighted distantly to leeward, but, said Dillon, "no notice was taken of it". This was truly extraordinary, for even if Howe himself was by that time worn out, it should have been Curtis's duty to send frigates ahead, to keep watch on the enemy. But Curtis was by that time preparing to speed home with dispatches, the harbinger of good news to that distant, summer England.

Meanwhile the *Defence* was hard at work getting up jury masts, the *Caesar*'s people helping. They now had time to view the prizes, the *Sans Pareil* of 80 guns, newly built and very speedy, *Le Juste* of the same weight of metal, and four 74's, *L'Impétueux*, *L'Achille*, *L'América* and the *Northumberland*, the latter ship named after a prize taken half a century before. Three of them had short lives under the British flag. *L'Impétueux* was accidentally blown up before the end of the year, and *L'Achille* and *Northumberland* went to the ship-breakers instead of being taken into service. *L'América*, which had been presented to France by the United States, was renamed *Impetuous* (later changed to *Impetueux*) in 1795, and served in the British navy almost throughout the war.

On 3rd June the *Defence* received fifty-six officers and men from the *Northumberland*. Some of the French seamen tried to get taken on as volunteers with the Royal Navy. "There was no end to their praises of our conduct and our victory," said Dillon, "but their offers were not accepted." As if to assure the reader that it was not prejudice which made him relate the story about West, and that foreigners—Revolutionary Frenchmen apart—were acceptable in the British ships, as was indeed the case, Dillon spoke of a

Swedish quartermaster who was at the wheel during the action, who behaved so admirably that "he was noticed by all the officers for his cool and determined bravery. He would have been a fit companion for Charles XII." His name was John Flemming, and he had been mate of an Indiaman.

Dillon noted one very odd circumstance concerning the *Leviathan*, which had served earlier with Samuel Hood at Toulon:

> "Whilst the French ship *América* was engaged with her," said Dillon, "the English ship pelted the enemy with silver dollars. . . . The hull of the *América*, on the side opposed to the *Leviathan*, was studded with pieces of silver. Some of the dollars were picked out of the planks."

Apparently, when at Toulon, the Captain, Lord Hugh Seymour, going the rounds of the dockyard, took a fancy to some fine brass howitzers. These were given to him and placed on his poop. Shot was needed:

> ". . . and some red tin canisters were sent with the guns, supposed to be belonging to them. . . . But the canisters, instead of containing grape shot, were filled with 5-franc French pieces. It was understood that the money belonged to some nobleman who had sent his property to the Dockyard as a place of safety during the Revolution, little thinking how it would be applied."

Later, Dillon was able to verify the fact with his own eyes.

After a day or two, the admiral sent to the ships for a return of casualties. Malcolm, the Surgeon in the *Defence*, had introduced flannel to the seamen "to protect them against the effects of rheumatism", but most unfortunately he could not amputate, which threw the whole burden of work on to his assistant, You-hall, an Irishman, who with the utmost cheerfulness and no little skill, worked twenty-two hours out of the twenty-four.

> "Many a time", said Dillon, "did I go the rounds with him and have witnessed his skill, and kind-hearted care of those brave men. I have known him come on the quarterdeck at 2 o'clock in the morning . . . to breathe some fresh air. He would then say: 'I have only two hours rest, after that, I must recommence my visits.'"

Gambier decided to omit the slightly wounded from his return. The ship had eighteen killed or died of wounds. Thirty-nine (out of a possible eighty) were notified as being wounded. Dillon, though still plastered and patched, was not among them.

> "Why, thought I, should not everyone who had received injury be reported to the Admiralty, that the Country might know those who had suffered in its cause?"

The reports were, in fact, made in so individual a fashion that it is difficult even now to know the cost of the engagement in human life. Captain Molloy, for instance, when his conduct came to be inquired into, produced some further casualties, not included in his original return, to show how much the *Caesar* had been involved. After careful sifting of the evidence, Professor Michael Lewis calculates the losses in the May-June actions as follows:*

British			French (in round figures)			
Killed	*Wounded*	*Total*	*Killed*	*Wounded*	*Total*	[Prisoners
287	811	1,098	1,500	2,000	3,500	3,500]

Some idea of the general vagueness concerning enemy loss is suggested in what Dillon heard. The prizes sent in returns of 690 killed and 580 wounded: they are suspicious proportions. Then the *Vengeur*, which sank after a famous duel with the *Brunswick*, Captain Harvey, reported 250 men saved, including the Captain and his son: "But", said Dillon, "it was supposed that ship lost 500 men, so that, in these same ships (i.e. the prizes and the *Vengeur*) there were 1,770 men killed, drowned and wounded. Therefore the total loss in the enemy's fleet, comparing them by these returns, must have been immense." Probably it was so, proportionately to the British, but a good guess is the best that can now be offered.

V

On 9th June, the *Caesar* relinquished her tow, and along came the frigate *Niger*, Captain Legge, "one of our favourite officers", Dillon remarked. The reason for the partiality soon appeared, for

* *A Social History of the Navy, 1793–1815* (1960).

Legge, by his seamanship, soon had the Fleet amazed. When he took over:

> ". . . on one occasion," said Dillon, "with a fine commanding breeze, he set all the studding sails that would draw, the wind being on the beam, and kept the hawser by which he held us so taut that Captain Gambier thought it must break. He accordingly hailed Captain Legge, requesting him to shorten sail; but in reply he told him 'Look out for being towed under water.' We were going at 7 knots. . . . The *Niger* in this instance made a most interesting appearance. All her sails were beautifully trimmed, and the ship gradually yielded over to the breeze, the yards all bending to the strain of the canvas. . . . Captain Legge continued his progress until the evening set in. We were then several miles ahead of the Fleet, and he shortened sail for the night.
>
> "This was, without exception, the finest sight I ever beheld of that nature."

On 11th June, old England was in sight, and that day Howe signalled for Admiral Graves, who had been badly wounded, to part company and proceed to Plymouth Sound, with the *Royal Sovereign, Impregnable, Marlborough, Tremendous, Gibraltar, Culloden, Alfred, Montagu* and *Orion*. The rest of the fleet, with the prizes, held on for Spithead.

Howe had sent Curtis ahead to give the country early news of victory, so that Portsmouth turned out in strength to welcome him. Howe had another taste of the vagaries of popular favour when the people insisted on chairing him to his hotel. The church bells rang out and at night the neighbourhood was "splendidly illuminated" with bonfires. Dillon, with some other midshipmen, thought it a good chance, while the *Defence* was in dockyard hands, to play some cricket. The team took two French officers with them, and a little comedy resulted.

> "One of the French officers, in attempting to catch the ball, hurt his hands. It was clear he did not understand what he was about", said Dillon, but noted that he intended to play on. "When he had to stop or catch the ball, he took off his hat for that purpose. Then, holding it on the ground as the missile came rolling along, it went slap through the crown. . . . What grimaces, with many a 'Sacré', then came out."

The game soon stopped, and the sailors consoled the prisoner with a drink. Next day, they gave him a new hat.

Dillon did not forget to go to Haslar Hospital, to see how the wounded were faring. They divided sharply, so he found, between the "mournful", who were not doing well, and the cheerful, who were still glorying over Howe's success. He found a former messmate who had been serving in Alexander Hood's flagship, the *Royal George*. He had lost a leg, and was attended by his mother, a lovely woman with a fine head of hair. Boys, the patient, was full of good cheer, bursting to tell Dillon how it had all happened.

> "He was enlarging on this subject," said Dillon, "when we were interrupted by another sufferer, a Mid who had also lost a leg, by his saying: 'Never mind the honour and glory of the Country. Give me my leg back again.' This poor fellow was dreadfully low-spirited. I therefore hastened to retire, after an affectionate adieu to my messmate."

On 26th June, King George III arrived from Windsor, attended by many of his family, with courtiers and ministers. He went on board the *Queen Charlotte* and presented Howe with a diamond-hilted sword of the value of 3,000 guineas.

When the King had gone, Howe stayed behind for some days, to entertain his captains, and to discuss the action with them. Dillon recorded one of Howe's rare jokes. Noticing the absence of Captain Payne of the *Russell*, Howe asked where he was. Nobody knew the answer, and Howe, sighing, said: he missed him, adding: "There is no pleasure without pain." Payne was a wag himself, for when he was first introduced to the Prince of Wales, H.R.H. said kindly: "If I mistake not, you have been bred to the sea." "Oh no, Sir," answered Payne, "the sea is bread to me, and damned hard bread, too!"

Dillon soon got leave of absence, and was lionised in London, though he became bored when his father insisted on his always appearing in uniform. "I could not move in the streets without being cheered," he said, "and many persons came and shook me by the hand. 'The Navy for ever' was constantly repeated. The whole nation was in a happy state of excitement.

Dillon's final claim to gratitude was that he went to see Mather Brown's well-known reconstruction of a scene on the quarterdeck of the *Queen Charlotte* at the time of the action, which was shown in Bond Street early the following year. It is an elaborate picture, made from sketches done at Spithead, and it includes among others Howe, Curtis, Sir Andrew Douglas, and Lieutenant Neville of the Queen's Royal Regiment, who died of wounds received in the action. But it did not please all tastes, least of all Bowen's. He complained at the inclusion of Hamond, a young relative of Sir Andrew Douglas, who was shown with a speaking trumpet under his arm, though his place in action was in the cockpit. Bowen had been asked to sit, so that his portrait should be included, but had refused if Hamond was to go in.

Dillon, with that eye for detail which distinguishes the seaman and sometimes annoys the artist, noticed that Mather Brown had painted the planks of the deck "so that they ran in an improper direction". So correct a young man should, perhaps, be given the last word.

5

The Case of Captain Collingwood

LORD HOWE apart, no officer in the Fleet won such distinction in the navy as Cuthbert Collingwood, flag-captain to Rear-Admiral Bowyer in the *Barfleur*. The admirals who took part, Graves, Alexander Hood, Bowyer, Gardner, Pasley and Caldwell, died or left the sea with creditable records, no more. Collingwood went on to take a noble share in the victory off Cape St. Vincent nearly three years later, and to succeed to Nelson's command after Trafalgar. To view the First of June through his eyes is to see glory—and then glory fading.

On 10th June, just before the fleet's return, Collingwood wrote to Dr. Alexander Carlyle, husband of his favourite aunt. He gave him such a succinct account of the actions as a whole that it is worth quoting, at the risk of repetition, in order to show how the engagements appeared at the time to a responsible officer in Howe's fleet. Collingwood saw with his usual clarity, busy as he was with his own ship's affairs, and with attending to his admiral, who had lost a leg.

> "We were three days engaged with them", he said, "before we could claim the victory. It was on the 28th of May we first met with them, they had 25 sail to our 26. Our advance squadron engaged their rear that evening and after dark took a three-decker of 100 guns. We in the body of the fleet knew nothing of this circumstance until two days after, as the *Audacious* immediately went off . . . for England."

Collingwood's description of the next phase shows that he and Admiral Bowyer appreciated Howe's intentions.

"On the 29th", Collingwood continued, "they did not decline action but wished to have it in their own way—at long shot— but Lord Howe by a very dexterous manœuvre tacked upon them, threw his whole force upon their rear, and cut them up very much. They retired to take care of their disabled ships, and our *Queen* and *Invincible,* having been roughly treated, wanted a good deal of making up."

Collingwood reported how the enemy had been joined by more ships, and then described how, having the weather-gage, the British line bore down on the 1st June:

"... with the signal for each ship to engage that opposed to her in the enemy's line close. Nothing could exceed the grandeur of the scene. In going down I observed to the admiral that notwithstanding their superior strength, in one thing we had very much the advantage of them—we should have the prayers of our wives for our success, whereas they had neither wives like ours, nor prayers to offer.

"About 10 the battle began from one end of the line to another, nearly at the same time: a more furious onset was never or more obstinately resisted. Before 12 they fled, leaving the seas covered with wreck and 7 noble ships to be captured by us."

Collingwood hoped that the battle would:

"... be attended by happy consequences, and tend to promote a peace; it certainly must give a security for our trade, which has lately suffered exceedingly. But is it not astonishing that the French, who we have despised, ruined in their finances, supplied with great difficulty with stores, and almost all Europe at war with them, should meet us at sea with a fleet superior to us? It is leaving too much to fortune and chance. Great as the skill of Lord Howe is, and we have nothing like him, it is not right to oppose us to a force that chance might give a victory to. I hope however their naval force is done for this summer; those that remain must be in a ruined and shattered state."

The captain of the *Barfleur* concluded with a tribute to his wounded admiral, "a very gallant and intelligent officer". Bowyer warmly returned the admiration, and within a few months had written to Lord Chatham to say so. He was in fact in a fair way of mending, and lived to enjoy the pleasures of the family seat at Radley Hall for some years to come. At one time he was said to haunt the main staircase.*

Collingwood wrote officially to Howe about the same time, in answer to his request for details about the action as seen by him in the *Barfleur*. At Bowyer's direction Collingwood had exchanged places in the line, on 1st June, with the *Invincible*, so that that rather battered two-decker should be faced with an opponent somewhere near to her own weight of metal. Collingwood praised her station-keeping.

> "The officers and ship's company of the *Barfleur*," he added, "displayed all that intrepid bravery which characterises Englishmen, preserving the most exact order, and reaped the advantage in that no accident happened but what was inevitable and the effect of the enemy's shot."

Collingwood included some further details in a letter written five days later to Sir Edward Blackett, his wife's uncle. Admiral Bowyer, he said,

> "Was so raised by the success of the day that he made his own misfortune of little consideration; and I believe he would have done himself material injury by his spirits if I had not at last shut him up and prohibited everybody but the surgeon and necessary attendants going near him. . . . It was early in the action that he was wounded by a great shot, and I caught him in my arms before he fell to the deck."

The first lieutenant was wounded in the head at the same time, but soon got himself patched up and returned to duty. Collingwood added that on the 1st June, as the British fleet closed, whereas the French fired at long range, "we reserved ours until we were so near that it was proper to cloud our ships in smoke. However, we were determined not to fire until Lord Howe had, and he is not in the habit of firing soon."

* Radley College continues the custom of flying the Union Flag above the Hall on 1st June, in Bowyer's honour.

II

After this letter, there came a cloud. Howe issued a statement naming certain officers as having particularly distinguished themselves in action—and Collingwood was not included. To a spirit like his, it was like a blow in the face.

This was not, emphatically, Howe's own fault. After the receipt of the news of his victory, Lord Chatham and the Board of Admiralty had replied in a formal letter to Howe, which was circulated and read to the officers and men of all ships concerned, stating the King's

> "... highest approbation of your spirited and judicious conduct and his highest satisfaction in the account you have given of the bravery and gallant behaviour of *all* the officers and men who were in action with you; and that it is also His Majesty's pleasure that you should, in the manner you judge most proper, acquaint *all* the officers and men, especially the admirals [all by name] with the just sense His Majesty entertains of the zeal and courage they have so eminently exerted in his service."

So far, so good: Howe himself would have preferred to have left it like that. But, so he told Lord Chatham, despite his "wearied mind" he was pressed to be more particular. He knew that the consequences might be unhappy.

> "Conscious, my lord," he wrote, "that almost every advantage to be derived from our late good fortune would be dependent on the general impression made by it, and the idea of perfect harmony subsisting in the fleet, as well as concurrent opinion of unexceptionable good conduct of every person having part in the late engagement, I wished to confine my reports to such general statement as I have given of our transactions. It was for these reasons I wished to have conversed with your lordship on the subject of framing some more confined narrative. But I am so assailed to name those officers who had opportunity of particularly distinguishing themselves, that I shall proceed with the earliest preparation of it, though I fear it may be followed by disagreeable consequences."

A more prophetic (or experienced) sentence than the last was never written, even by Howe. When he was First Lord he had

19 *Captain Payne of
the "Russell"*

*From an enamel
miniature by Henry Bone
hitherto unpublished*

20 *Lord Hugh Seymour,
of the "Leviathan"*

*From the portrait by
John Hoppner*

21 *Captain Collingwood,*
    of the "Barfleur"

Detail of the portrait by
Henry Howard

22 *Admiral Gardner*

Detail of the portrait by
Theophilus Clarke

once remarked that patronage was not nearly as desirable as might be supposed. There were usually twenty candidates for every appointment. In choosing, a First Lord was certain to disappoint nineteen, and by no means invariably pleased the twentieth.

Struggling with a problem to which he saw no happy solution, he wrote to Chatham a few days later to say that he had:

"... endeavoured to satisfy the expectations for a more particular detail of the services the *apparently* most distinguished commanders in the fleet performed on the late occasion."

Privately, he added that he still felt so fatigued that:

"... I must beg you will allow me to refer you to Sir Roger Curtis for any particulars you may desire to be informed of which are unnoticed, respecting the late operations."

Howe's original observations had been published in the *London Gazette Extraordinary* dated 11th June, and after noting that a commander-in-chief of a fleet was unavoidably so confined in his view that he could seldom bear personal testimony to those who did well, he said that he had called for reports from the various flag-officers serving under his command on the conduct of those who were in their divisions. As a result of this call:

"Those officers ... who have particular claim to my attention are, the Admirals Graves and Sir Alexander Hood; the Rear-Admirals Bowyer, Gardner and Pasley; the Captains Lord Hugh Seymour, Pakenham, Berkeley, Gambier, John Harvey, Payne, Parker, Henry Harvey, Pringle, Duckworth and Elphinstone. Special notice is also due of the Captains Nicholls of the *Sovereign* and Hope of the *Bellerophon*, who became charged with, and well conducted, those ships when the wounded flag officers, under whom they respectively served therein, were no longer able to remain at their posts; and the Lieutenants Monkton of the *Marlborough* and Donnelly of the *Montagu*, in similar situations."

There was a "saving clause" which, however, consoled no one who had had his name omitted:

"These selections", wrote Howe, "should not be construed to the disadvantage of other commanders, who may have been equally deserving of the approbation of the Lords Commissioners of the

Admiralty, although I am not enabled to make a particular statement of their merits."

The original *Gazette* had noticed Sir Roger Curtis and Sir Andrew Douglas, as was only to be expected, the officers concerned being under Howe's own eye. The *Supplementary Gazette* was instantly attributed to Sir Roger Curtis, Collingwood saying that it was only one more instance of his trying to make out that everything had been done by the *Queen Charlotte*.

In Collingwood's words, addressed on 30th June to Sir Edward Blackett:

"Lord Howe's supplemental letter threw the fleet into the utmost consternation and astonishment. There was not a cool heart amongst us before except Molloy's, whose conduct is past defence, and though the situation of the ships in so large a fleet must necessarily be very different on such a day, there was not, I believe, a suspicion in the mind of any man that all had not done their duty well.

"The appearance of that letter nearly broke my heart . . . ."

Well it might, for his omission, when Bowyer was mentioned with honour, was quite inexcusable.

The only other case where a captain might have felt a grievance, nearly, though not quite equal to Collingwood's was that of William Domett of the *Royal George*, whose admiral, Alexander Hood, received honourable mention. But Hood had not left Domett the direction of affairs, as had Bowyer to Collingwood owing to a serious wound.

To add to his chagrin, Collingwood must have noticed that, while the admirals were duly placed in order of seniority, with the captains it was not so. To have attempted what appeared to be an order of merit among the meritorious seemed adding insult to injury. Seldom had an official letter of praise been issued with so little satisfaction.

As soon as he was free to do so, Collingwood went to Curtis to protest, and to ask to see Lord Howe. Curtis put him off, and said,

". . . 'no disapprobation was meant to be implied, but that in the selection the Admiral was pleased to make, he must stop somewhere, and the good conduct of the fleet was summed up in a later sentence.' All that could be said to that", added Collingwood, "was that it was a most unfortunate style. Those who were mentioned in this letter were almost as much offended at the manner as those who were omitted."

In fact, if any selection were made, it could scarcely have failed to be invidious, but Collingwood was certainly the most glaring omission. The other captains not specifically referred to, Pigott of the *Tremendous*, Mackenzie of the *Gibraltar*, Bazely of the *Alfred*, Cotton of the *Majestic*, Bertie of the *Thunderer*, Schomberg of the *Culloden*, and Rear-Admiral Caldwell and his captain, Westcott, in the *Impregnable*, certainly had a less arduous share in the fighting: but they all—except the *Thunderer*—had action casualties, and the officers and men of the ships whose captains were omitted must necessarily have felt the reflection not only on their commanders but on their ships.

What made matters worse was that captains were not invited on board the *Queen Charlotte* when the King presented Howe with the diamond sword, though they escorted the Sovereign to the fleet flagship in their barges, and Collingwood (sparing Howe), attributed all slights to Curtis, who, he said:

"... ever has been an artful, sneaking creature, whose fawning, insinuating manners creep into the confidence of whoever he attacks, and whose rapacity would grasp all honours and profits that come within his view."

These were strong, even passionate, words, but the King's visit had a somewhat happier ending:

"Lord Hugh Seymour", said Collingwood, "represented to Lord Howe how justly the officers of the fleet were dissatisfied with their treatment: they had hoped that when His Majesty did them the honour to hoist his flag in the fleet, they should not have been by order excluded from his presence; that nothing could have been more gratifying to them than to witness the honours conferred on *him*, which he had so justly merited ... and he knew of no honour the officers of the Navy had received by his presence unless sitting in a boat for hours was an honour."

Lord Howe defended himself as well as he could, and said he would remain in the fleet no longer than he could give general satisfaction. Moreover, amends were made.

> "We have been introduced to the King and Queen," said Collingwood, "and had the honour of kissing hands. . . . On Sunday we all dined with His Majesty, and, surpassing my expectation, had a very pleasant day. He was cheerful and good humoured to all, and there was as little ceremony as at the table of a private gentleman."

But, as the months passed, the omission of his name still rankled with Collingwood. He continued to prefer to serve with Howe, whom he thoroughly respected, but said to Dr. Carlyle: "It would be a sweet sort of revenge, to exact from him that justice which he has withheld, and if it please God, that day will come."

It came on St. Valentine's Day, 1797, when Collingwood, then commanding H.M.S. *Excellent*, fought his ship superlatively against the Spaniards. The captains in the fleet were all, without exception, awarded gold medals. Collingwood said to the Commander-in-Chief that he could not consent to receive his, while that for the First of June was withheld. "I feel", he said, "that I was then improperly passed over; and to receive such a distinction now would be to acknowledge the propriety of that injustice." Lord St. Vincent understood: "That is precisely the answer I expected from you, Captain Collingwood," he said.

As a result of representations, Collingwood was sent two gold medals, one for each action, and each appropriately inscribed. Honour was satisfied, justice done.

III

In the other sad, though very different case—that of Molloy—the ending was less happy. As Molloy was a friend of Curtis, Howe himself would have preferred to say no more about his conduct in action, at a time of general rejoicing. But Collingwood's view, that he was "past defence" was so general, that Molloy found himself shunned by his fellow captains. He went through such an agony of mind that he felt his name could only be cleared as the result of a court-martial. Howe tried to dissuade him from seeking one, but he was adamant. Nearly a year after the battle, the Court was held on board the *Glory* at Portsmouth. The result was that Molloy was sentenced to be dismissed from the *Caesar* for not having done his utmost to bring his ship into close action on 29th May and 1st June 1794. It also found that Molloy's courage had been unimpeachable on these occasions. As so often was the case, the "saving clause" brought no satisfaction, and Molloy was never again employed at sea.

6

Ships in Battle

THERE ARE fuller accounts of the proceedings of some British
ships at the First of June than of others. Many records are confined—as in the case of the *Barfleur*, for example—mainly to a
note of times, weather, signals and bald facts, though Collingwood,
in the report which he made on Bowyer's behalf, gave the reason
why, even in certain cases where Howe's signal to break through
the French line and engage them from leeward was fully understood, it could not always be obeyed. "We found it impracticable
to pass to leeward", he said simply, "without interrupting the fire
of the ships ahead of us, and in danger of being fired into by them."

Howe's fleet was organised into Van, Centre and Rear
Squadrons, in a manner familiar from the wars of the seventeenth
century. Graves commanded the van in the *Royal Sovereign*,
having under him two divisions, Pasley's, who flew his flag in the
Bellerophon, Captain Hope, and Caldwell's, flag in the *Impregnable*,
Captain Westcott. Pasley's included the fastest ships, Molloy's
Caesar, his own *Bellerophon*, Payne's *Russell* and Berkeley's
Marlborough, all of which did well except the first. All but the
Caesar were 74's. And it reflects on Molloy that Pasley preferred to
fly his flag in the *Bellerophon* rather than in the most powerful ship
in his division. Had the Admiral been where he seemed to belong,
the record of the day might have been even brighter than it was.

Graves' second division included Parker's *Audacious*, Gambier's
Defence, Caldwell's three-decked *Impregnable*, Schomberg's *Culloden*
and Pigott's *Tremendous*.

Howe's centre was also in two divisions. The first included

Pakenham's *Invincible*, the *Barfleur*, with Bowyer's flag, and Mackenzie's *Gibraltar*. In the second division was the *Brunswick*, commanded by John Harvey, the *Valiant*, Captain Pringle, the *Orion*, Captain Duckworth, and the *Queen*, with Gardner's flag.

Sir Alexander Hood commanded the two divisions of the rear squadron. In the first was the *Ramillies*, commanded by Henry Harvey (brother of the captain of the *Brunswick*), the *Alfred*, Captain Bazely, Hood's own *Royal George*, successor to Kempenfelt's famous ship which had sunk at Spithead twelve years before, and the *Montagu*, commanded by an officer of the same name, brother of the admiral detached on convoy duty. Captain Montagu was killed in the action. The second division included the *Majestic*, Captain Cotton, the three-decked *Glory*, Captain Elphinstone, and the *Thunderer*, Captain Bertie.

The frigates, whose duties were to reconnoitre, to repeat signals, to keep in touch with the enemy during the night, reporting their movements, and to remain on the disengaged side of the fleet when the big ships were in action, ready to assist as necessary, were the *Latona*, Captain Thornbrough; the *Niger*, Captain Legge, which served as repeating frigate for the van; the *Venus*, Captain Brown; the *Aquilon*, Captain Stopford, repeating frigate for the rear; the *Phaeton*, Captain Bentinck; the *Southampton*, Captain Forbes, and the *Pegasus*, Captain Barlow, repeating frigate for the centre. Also accompanying the fleet were two fireships, the *Comet* and *Incendiary*, a hospital ship, the *Charon*, and two cutters, the *Rattler* and *Ranger*.

Howe was well served by his lighter vessels, and he would have liked his frigate captains to have received consideration when honours were awarded. This was not the custom of the time, and he did not have his way, but the action is recorded, together with any other notable service, on scrolls of honour, by ships succeeding to their names.

II

By good fortune, Captain Hope of the *Bellerophon*, whose place in the formal order of sailing was second to the *Caesar*, kept a journal. It is well that he did so, for the ship was one of the most famous 74's of her time, and she was afloat from 1786 for fifty years. She was later conspicuous at the Battle of the Nile, where she engaged the French commander-in-chief; she was in the line at Trafalgar, where her captain was killed, and in 1815, after Waterloo, she had the distinction of conveying Napoleon to Plymouth. It was particularly fitting that a ship which was in the first great action of the war should have had a hand in its conclusion. Pasley, flying his flag in her, started a series of battle honours which was enviably maintained. Her junior officers included Matthew Flinders, later a well-known hydrographer, who recorded in a private journal that all Howe's signals were perfectly understood in the *Bellerophon*, though he observed that it did not seem to be so with other ships. He also noted that Pasley was hit by "an 18-pounder shot which came through the barricadoes on the quarter-deck".

It was about 3 o'clock on 28th May, the weather "fresh gales and squally, with showers and a heavy swell from [the] westward", when the *Bellerophon* saw the *Russell* fire the first ranging shots at the *Révolutionnaire* and other French ships. The *Bellerophon*, by skilled manœuvring, was soon in action herself, and Howe, seeing her engaged with a three-decker—usually considered the equal of at least two 74's—signalled the *Russell* and *Marlborough* to go to her help, the *Caesar* being then away to leeward (well beyond harm). The *Leviathan* and *Thunderer* were also in action, and soon up came the *Audacious*, whose guns silenced the big Frenchman. By that time the *Bellerophon* had been knocked about, and she had to signal inability to continue in action: but she had tasted blood, and next day she followed Howe in breaking through the enemy line.

> "In passing," said Captain Hope, "we brought down a ship's topmast, and in the heat of the action it was difficult to know who was French or who was English, we was all firing through one another. . . . In passing the line we had our sails and rigging cut to pieces. . . . At night, thick, foggy weather."

On 30th May, at eight in the morning, Captain Hope saw the

enemy to leeward, four or five miles away; then the fog closed. When it cleared on the afternoon of the 31st, the French were about double the distance. That night, the *Phaeton* went along Howe's line, hailed the different ships, and said it was the Admiral's intention to carry his foresail, single-reefed topsails, jib and main topmast staysail all night. This information gave the captains an idea of the speed of his advance, and they regulated their own movements accordingly.

Hope's record of 1st June shows that at first light—"fresh breezes and cloudy"—the enemy was not everywhere visible, and that the British rear was a long way from the van. The signal was made—and repeated—for the fleet to close, and at about 6 o'clock the French were seen to the northward. About 8 o'clock, Villaret-Joyeuse closed up his line. Then, said Hope:

> "... about ½ past 8 ran down on the enemy in nearly a line abreast, with the signal for close action, and each ship to engage his opponent in the line. Ran down and lay upon our opponent's quarter within muskett shot, in going down we received a very heavy fire from 3 or 4 of the enemy's van. At 50 minutes past 10 the Admiral unfortunately lost his leg"—at much the same time as Bowyer lost his—"before which ... we had once or twice made the *Caesar*'s signal for close action, she lying frequently to windward of us."

By noon, the *Bellerophon* had lost her topmasts, and most of her shrouds were shot away. She signalled the *Latona* to take her in tow, and then began the work of repair. Hope noted that although some of the French were dismasted, they still continued firing, and he also saw the danger that the *Queen* and *Brunswick*, both badly damaged and to leeward, appeared to be in. He also remarked the brave handling of Villaret-Joyeuse's flagship *Montagne*. She was:

> "... to windward, by herself, keeping up an incessant fire on the ships as they passed. She then bore round, set her foresail and joined the remainder of the fleet. By this time the French ships that were not disabled formed a kind of line to leeward, stood to the eastward and fired on our ships as they passed, particularly the *Queen*, who had only her foremast standing."

Admiral Pasley, from his cot, was able to sign a letter to Howe about the actions. He was forthright in his remarks about some of the captains, including particularly Mackenzie of the *Gibraltar* and Molloy of the *Caesar*. Of the encounter on the 29th May he said:

> "On that day, and for some days before, the *Bellerophon* was the worst-sailing ship of the flying squadron. Yet by embracing the moment for tacking after the enemy, she was enabled to bring them to action, with which she was engaged alone more than an hour and a half."

Full of praise as Pasley was for his flagship and the *Bellerophon*'s ship's company, the admiral felt so strongly about certain other ships that he said he would like to have discussed their conduct with Howe in person, which was at present impossible.

> "How it came to pass I cannot tell," he said, "but on 1st June the *Tremendous* was observed from the *Bellerophon* lying before the *Leviathan*'s quarter and was three-quarters of a mile to windward of that ship. I made her signal at 35 minutes past 10, which she answered at 54 minutes past 10 with a signal of inability. The *Tremendous* did not appear to be damaged in masts, sails or yards."

According to her captain, the *Tremendous* was damaged, and it must have been hard for Pasley to judge a distant ship's true condition in the heat of action.

As for the *Caesar*, in Pasley's view, she was beyond redemption, though, said Pasley, "I make no doubt but Captain Molloy will explain to you the reasons for his conduct". Molloy was Irish, a nation in whom words of justification rarely fail.

Pasley was not merely condemnatory. Besides the *Bellerophon*'s people, whom he observed with admiration, he considered that Lord Hugh Seymour in the *Leviathan* and Captain Payne in the *Russell* "deserve my warmest praise, particularly the former who supported me most gallantly during the whole of the battle".

III

Of the *Leviathan*, her captain, Lord Hugh Seymour, frankly confessed to Howe that his officers had been too busy to keep a proper log. This was probably true of many other ships, but it was seldom so honestly stated.

The ship was firing for about an hour on 28th May, at a ship near the *Révolutionnaire*. Seymour, realising the importance of noting and signalling Villaret-Joyeuse's movements during the night, tried to keep in touch with the French fleet, but, he said in his circumstantial letter to Howe: "I am apprehensive that from the number of lights shown on board different ships between us (i.e. between the *Leviathan* and the flagship), I did not succeed."

In the action on 29th May the *Leviathan* had her wheel "knocked to pieces by a shot" and she was thereafter steered by relieving tackles. Seymour observed with admiration the conduct of his "gallant leader", Pasley in the *Bellerophon*, on 1st June. As for his own ship's company, their conduct was:

> "... the most perfect that can be imagined ... from the beginning to the end of the business in which we have been engaged; every wish of mine has been accomplished as far as depended upon their exertions and upon their spirit."

Of the *Russell*, next in the line, not much is recorded, though her Captain, Payne, fought with valour. But Mr. Stewart, Master of the *Marlborough*, the last in Pasley's division, kept a detailed journal, and the ship's record was sufficiently memorable for incidents in her fighting to be included by Sir John Barrow in his life of Howe.

A note of the engagement of 29th May shows the meticulous discipline which Howe expected of his fleet. He seldom held councils of captains at sea, preferring to manage everything on his own responsibility, relying on his signal book to convey his exact meaning. Whenever necessary, he repeated signals with a gun, especially if they were not acknowledged or acted upon swiftly. His orders were so precise that on 29th May the Master noted that "ships were at liberty to fire on the enemy, though not meant to bring them to general action immediately". This was Signal No. 28, made generally to the Fleet, and is an indication of the firm control which Howe intended to keep of every phase of encounter. A little later the log records that an order to "tack in succession" was repeated by the firing of a gun. Next day there was a general signal: "Interrogating to know if the fleet is in order to renew the battle. Answered affirmative by *Marlborough* and fleet. *Caesar* made signal of inability to comply." So did the *Bellerophon*, whose damage from the early fighting had been extensive.

Mr. Stewart was among those who remarked that, on 1st June, it was the *Defence* which first came under fire. The action itself is recorded graphically, if tersely.

> "9.45 The *Marlborough* began to engage the enemy. 9.47 *Royal Sovereign* made signal to engage close. . . . 9.55 Broke through the French line, passed close under our opponent's stern and engaged him to leeward. 10.02 Our opponent ran on board us on the larboard quarter. Soon after another ship of the enemy attempted to board us, which our heavy fire prevented, and he ran on board our opponent. 10.15 Our opponent carried away his bowsprit over our quarter and soon after his fore mast, also his main and mizzen masts and lay a perfect wreck. Not a man to be seen at his quarters.
>
> "Some of our people having boarded him, the other ship which was on board of our opponent's quarter (luffing up) boarded the *Marlborough* on the larboard bow, where he lay totally dismasted by the *Marlborough*.
>
> "Shortly after a French 3-decker came under our stern, and having his main topsail to the mast, raked us, which wounded Captain Berkeley severely, carried away our three masts and did us other considerable damage. Observed the *Gibraltar* and *Culloden* firing at us, probably by mistaking our St. George's ensign for the national flag. . . . 11.40 Made the signal for assistance but it was almost immediately shot away."

It is sad that the journal records another stupidity on the part of the *Gibraltar*, but it makes clear the difficulty of recognition, for Captain Schomberg in the *Culloden* was an alert and intelligent officer. The fact was that Villaret-Joyeuse's fleet had not yet all been issued with the new French Tricolour, which made things simpler in later battles.

Captain Berkeley and his first lieutenant, Monkton, were both mentioned in Howe's letter of praise. Berkeley, in a letter quoted in Barrow, says that one of the *Marlborough*'s immediate opponents was *L'Impétueux* and that some of his men actually boarded her, but were called back. Monkton added details.

> "At the time Captain Berkeley was obliged to quit the deck," he said, "we were still on board [i.e. entangled with the French ships] but backing clear of our opponents; our masts then being shot away by the three-decker under our stern, carried away the ensign staff and deprived us of hoisting any colours for a few minutes.
>
> "I ordered the wreckage to be cleared away from the colour chest and spread a Union Jack at the spritsail yard and a St. George's [i.e. White] ensign at the stump of the foremast; but perceiving that the latter was mistaken by some of our own ships for the tri-coloured flag, I ordered the [fly of the] flag to be cut off.
>
> "At this time we were laying along *L'Impétueux,* within pistol shot; and, finding that she did not return a gun, and perceiving she was on fire, I ordered our ship to cease firing at her, and suffered them quietly to extinguish the flames, which I could easily have prevented with our musketry."

The *Marlborough* was soon in danger from another quarter altogether.

> "While clearing away the wreckage," continued Monkton, "the rear of the enemy's fleet was coming up, and perceiving that they must range close to us, and being determined never to see the British flag struck, I ordered the men to lie down at their quarters to receive their fire, and to return it afterwards if possible, but being dismasted, she rolled so deep that our lower deck ports could not be opened.
>
> "The event was as I expected: the enemy's rear passed us to leeward very close, and we fairly ran the gauntlet of every ship which could get a gun to bear, but luckily without giving us any shots between wind and water, or killing any men, except two who unfortunately disobeyed their officers and got up at their quarters."

The *Marlborough*'s practice of making the men lie down when not serving their guns was typical of all fleets in which Howe commanded. It was not, unfortunately, universal practice, and Southey, in his *Life of Nelson,* records details of unnecessary slaughter at Copenhagen—supplied to him by his brother, who was there—from not following Howe's example. This was all the sadder, because the men concerned were soldiers serving with Hyde Parker's fleet.*

IV

The last ship to be considered in Pasley's division, the *Caesar* would deserve little notice but for the passage in the minutes of the court-martial on her captain which shows him in a predicament at once mortifying and dramatic—if it is strictly true.

In earlier engagements Molloy reported having continuous difficulty through the splitting of sails. More trouble awaited him. On 1st June:

> "... at ¼ past 8 bore up per signal to attack our opponent in the enemy's line", he said. "At 12 minutes past 9, the three van ships of the enemy's line began firing upon us, the 4 and 5 firing at the *Bellerophon*, who appeared to me to be close alongside the fourth ship but standing on towards their van.
>
> "At 25 minutes past 9, backed the main topsail, and opened our fire on the van ship of the enemy's line, upon which their second ship closed to the first, and both ships kept a heavy fire upon us, which we returned as quick as possible."

There is no mention of distance, but the fire was evidently at a fairly long range, contrary to Howe's instructions.

> "A short time after," said Molloy, "not seeing our opponent for the smoke, I ceased firing; and as it cleared away I observed that they had edged down from us and increased their distance. I therefore ordered the mizen topsail to be backed and the helm to be put hard to port, and told the master (who was at the conn) to steer close down on the weather bow of the van ship."

Then came an incident of which Molloy made much—the damage to his ship by enemy fire.

> "The men at the wheel at that moment called out that the rudder was chocked and that they could not move it either way. We then squared our foreyard, and lay with our three topsails to the mast. Our signal was at that instant made by the *Bellerophon* to come to

* The 49th Regiment and one company of Manningham's Corps of Riflemen (later the Rifle Brigade).

close action; our mizen yard was shot in two and the mizenmast quite through and through, and we expected every moment it would fall. In this extreme awkward position we lay for more than thirty minutes with our signal flying to come to closer action."

It was a time of crowning humiliation. If the *Caesar* had done well in the earlier actions, she might have been excused. As it was, every captain jumped to the worst conclusions.

"I want words to express the pain and anxiety I laboured under all the time", continued Molloy. "The carpenter, master and three lieutenants went to examine the cause of the obstruction of the rudder, and the carpenter reported to me that two shot had struck the rudder, one of which was lodged between the sternpost and the rudder. . . . Soon after we discovered that a shot had driven a splinter and a part of one of the lower deck port ropes into the starboard quarter block of the tiller rope, which had jammed the rope in the sheave."

The matter was soon put to rights, and the *Caesar* then "bore round upon the van ship of the enemy". There was no doubt what the men felt about going into closer action.

"In the eagerness of their joy," said Molloy, "which I could not restrain, they ran on deck on the booms and starboard gangway, and gave three cheers, during which time the second ship of the van fired at us and wounded several men. I ordered the people to return to their quarters and we backed close down on the second ship, but we had scarce fired on her, when she also bore away with as much sail as she could set."

The battle was in fact nearly over, and Molloy soon saw a signal flying in the *Royal Sovereign*, about half a mile to leeward, for ships to close round. Molloy obeyed.

His ship had had much damage. She had been struck by sixty-four shot, and had seven guns disabled, including a 24-pounder which, in bursting, had killed two men and wounded three others. But she had not closed as she should have done, and her total casualty list, eighteen killed and thirty-seven wounded, brought her little sympathy from ships which had obeyed orders with zeal and alacrity.

23 *"The Evening of the Glorious First of June"*
Engraved by T. Medland from a painting by Robert Cleveley, 1795

24　*Contemporary model of the "Queen Charlotte's" stern. Lord Howe's*
"great cabin" is immediately below that of the captain.
The lower row of windows are those of the ward-room

If he had been unable to take much part himself, Molloy had at least a befitting admiration for others.

> "The only observations I made during the action", he said, "were of the very spirited and noble conduct of Rear-Admiral Pasley and Lord Hugh Seymour, the *Bellerophon* and *Leviathan* being the only ships I took notice of during the whole of the action."

There is also this to be said. When the *Caesar* was at Spithead after the battle, gossip began to spread to the press. As a result, the officers sent the following letter to a newspaper: it was dated 27th June and it was signed by sea-officers and marines alike.

> "Having seen a paragraph in the public newspapers, reflecting on the character and conduct of Captain Molloy ... in the late actions with the French fleet, we feel it a duty incumbent on us as Officers and Gentlemen, to say, that his conduct in those several days of 28th and 29th of May, and of the 1st of this present month, was that of a man of the strictest courage, and appeared to those officers more immediately stationed near his person to be zealous in support of his country and the British flag."

Those words carried weight in his support, when Molloy's conduct came to be enquired into.

V

In the second division of the van, led by Admiral Graves in the *Royal Sovereign*, was the *Audacious*, Captain William Parker. Although in action only on 28th May, he fought with enough distinction to be mentioned in Howe's *Supplementary Gazette*. This was all the more creditable as it came at the end of a long chase to windward, in failing light.

Parker, who like Collingwood later served with honour at the Battle of Cape St. Vincent, was for some two hours in close action, "never exceeding the distance of half a cable's length [i.e. 100 yards] ... but generally closer" and in an awkward sea. *Le Révolutionnaire* seems to have attempted to close and board, but then ran before the wind.

"When the enemy separated from athwart our bows," said Parker, "the company of his Majesty's ship under my command gave three cheers, from the idea, taken from the people quartered forward, that his colours were struck. This I cannot myself take upon me to say, though I think it likely, from his situation obliging him to pass through or near our line. But certain it is he was completely broken; his fire slackened towards the latter part of the action, and the last broadside (the ship's sides almost touching each other) he sustained without returning more than the fire of two or three guns."

The *Audacious* lay to for the night, which was very dark. "People all night splicing and reeving new running rigging," said a justly-proud captain, hoping to make sure of a capture in the morning. His luck was out.

"Soon after daylight," said Parker "to our utmost chagrin and astonishment, we discovered nine sail of the enemy's ships about three miles to windward."

Moreover, there was no support in sight. At a little after 5 a.m. the look-outs:

"... saw the ship we engaged lying without any masts standing, only the bowsprit and spritsail yard hanging up and down, a complete hulk."

French prisoners taken earlier in the cruise reported *Le Révolutionnaire* as having been called the *Bretagne* in the days of the Royalist Navy, and they said she carried 110 guns. The danger to the now isolated *Audacious* was soon apparent.

"Bent a new foresail," said Mr. Louthear, the Master, "main topsail and mizen staysail. Two ships of the enemy's line bearing down and standing after us. Made what sail we could afore the wind."

Further alarm came at half-past nine.

"Three ships to windward came down, and proved to be 1 frigate and two corvettes of the enemy. Got our guns to bear and fired on them. . . . At 50 minutes past 10, the above frigate began to fire on us. Returned the fire. At noon the above vessels hauled their wind to the eastward. Got a new fore topsail on the top ready to bend. Ships chasing us astern, now out of sight."

Danger was now past. Under her new sails the *Audacious* was able to reach England well ahead of her friends. Parker had intended to anchor at Plymouth but "the wind was too scanty to allow of fetching this port". Off the Lizard, as already noted, Parker spoke with Captain Curzon of the frigate *Pallas*, belonging to Admiral Montagu's squadron, and gave him letters for both Montagu and the Admiralty. In his letter to their Lordships, Parker particularly praised:

> "Lieutenant Crofton of the 69th Regiment whose alertness and activity with his men at small arms in supporting the seamen arm'd to defend the boarding (which occurr'd twice during the Action) gave me perfect satisfaction." He added: "The conduct of my ship's company, from the greater part of them never in His Majesty's service before, and scarcely any ever in action, exceeded every possible expectation: as also the soldiers of the 69th Regiment who were all young recruits a twelve month ago when they were embarked on board."

The officers and men of the *Audacious*, together with her gallant soldiers, were among the earliest people to hear the news which Curtis brought of the encounter fought on the previous Sunday, and they were there to welcome their friends when the rest of the fleet anchored.

VI

Neither Rear-Admiral Caldwell in the *Impregnable*, nor Captain Pigott in the *Tremendous*, played an outstanding part in the May-June engagements, though Caldwell was at least never accused of "shyness". He was perhaps merely unlucky. He certainly believed himself to have been deliberately slighted in not obtaining a mention in Howe's letter of praise, but this is in fact unlikely. Howe expected much of his three-decked ships, and of the seven in his fleet, the *Impregnable* had the lightest casualties (7 killed and 21 wounded) and she was not remarked upon by other ships for prowess in action.

The *Impregnable* lost her three topgallant masts and had her foreyard shot away in the slings—which indicates that she received her damage at fairly long range: and among such dashing divisional admirals as Gardner, Bowyer and Pasley, Caldwell seems colourless. And yet he had served with distinction twelve years before, when commanding the *Agamemnon* under Rodney at the Battle of the Saints, and earlier with Kempenfelt, and in his own account of the First of June, forwarded to Howe as a letter of Observations and Proceedings, he reported that for much of the earlier part of the action he closed to a cable's length. He did not, however, explain why he did not attempt to break through the French line with his massive ship.

There is, moreover, an entry in a Minute of Proceedings forwarded by Caldwell which escaped the attention of earlier commentators on the battle, and which may explain at least something of Howe's apparently cool attitude to Collingwood.

p.m. First
of June

COMMENT BY LORD HOWE

N.B. No such signal made in the *Queen Charlotte*. But appeared to have been made by the Captain of the *Barfleur* when Rear-Admiral Bowyer was wounded, through inattention to the times and words of the instruction referred to.

Impregnable: *Proceedings*

Moderate breezes and clear weather. Our ship nearly unmanageable from the state of her Masts, Yards, Sails and Rigging. Exchanged fire with two of the Enemy's Line passing to Windward.

At 1 Lord Howe made the signal to open secret instructions—at about 2 the *Venus* hailed saying "It was the Admiral's order to keep in closer line of battle".

In the mass of original documents on this and later battles, assembled by the Admiralty in 1859 and presented to the British Museum (*Add. Ms. 23,207*), this underlining and comment is the only one in Howe's own unmistakable hand. His irritation at the mistake (if indeed it was Collingwood's), would have been natural. Signalling was Howe's special care, and for captains to have been distracted in battle by opening secret instructions—which usually referred to the rendezvous to be kept if and when ships become separated—would have gone counter to all his principles.

Caldwell was in other respects oddly out of touch. It was not until after the main battle was over that he noticed that the *Audacious* was missing, and the *Tremendous*, in his division, drew repeated comment (from Pasley among others) for her poor response to signals.

How soon gunfire shrouded a naval engagement is shown by a remark of Caldwell's to the effect that:

> "From 9.25 a.m. on 1st June (at which time we repeated Lord Howe's general signal to engage the enemy closer, and kept it flying most of the action) to 10.40 when we ceased firing a short time, no signal could be seen by the *Impregnable*. That interval admitted of seeing Lord Howe's general signal to make more sail. No other signal was seen till we observed the *Royal Sovereign* with the general signal to chase."

The *Royal Sovereign*'s signal was made on the initiative of Captain Nicholls, since Admiral Graves was by that time wounded and below. It was soon annulled. The ships which had distinguished themselves in battle were in no state to obey it—and the rest, on their showing in action, would have been unlikely to chase with effect.

The star ships in the second division were Admiral Graves's own *Royal Sovereign*, and Gambier's *Defence*, whose exploits have already been recorded.

In the *Royal Sovereign*, Graves had been wounded by ten o'clock and was obliged to leave the deck, but he ordered Nicholls, his flag-captain, to act in his place, which Nicholls did with coolness and address. A note in the ship's Letter of Proceedings, addressed to Howe after the battle, says:

> "N.B. The time after 40 minutes past Nine is probably not very correct, as the Person appointed to take Minutes was then killed."

The note, signed by John Blake, the Fourth Lieutenant, indicates that the same broadside which wounded Graves killed "the Person" referred to.

In Bowyer's division, the first of the centre, the *Barfleur* herself and Pakenham's *Invincible* did well: though the *Invincible*'s Master, Mr. Long, was even more laconic in his log than most of his fellow Masters. One of the most interesting records was left by Captain Schomberg of the *Culloden*, who composed a valuable note of Observations and Proceedings.

Isaac Schomberg was an efficient but unlucky officer. Eight years before, as an experienced lieutenant, he had been appointed to the frigate *Pegasus* as wet-nurse to the young Prince William Henry, afterwards William IV. The *Pegasus* was the Prince's first command. In the course of a cruise in the West Indies Schomberg fell foul of his autocratic captain, and was placed under arrest, in a sticky climate, for weeks on end. He had been relieved in due course, but sympathies in the navy generally seem to have been with him, for he soon gained promotion under Cornwallis on the East Indies station.

In the Atlantic fighting, Schomberg had only a distant view of the *Audacious* on the evening of 28th May, but the Master of his ship confirmed how close Parker had been at grips with *Le Révolutionnaire*, so much so that it was apparent that boarding had been attempted. The importance of this incident was that it set a good example. The French had been actively encouraged by Saint-André to board. The British, or at any rate the bolder among them, took to it naturally. The long-range gunfire captains were in a minority.

On 31st May, the day of fog and waiting, seems to have been a restless one in the *Culloden*. "Punished Richard Alfred and Dan Malone with 18 lashes for fighting", records the Master's log, without comment of any kind. "Ditto Pat Sullivan for striking the ship's corporal." There is in fact one other incident recording floggings, which took place in the frigate *Latona*. This time they were for disobedience, insolence and contempt. These occurred the day after the battle and not, as in the case of the *Culloden*, just before it. The *Culloden* was not, in fact, a happy ship and her people mutinied before the end of the year, though by that time they had another captain.

The *Culloden* had her difficulties in keeping her appointed place in the line, for on 15th June she was hailed by the *Barfleur* and told by Collingwood, on Bowyer's orders, "to drop into her station and preserve the line as exactly as she could that she might keep out of the line of the fire". The log comments: "made and shortened sail occasionally to keep in our station". The difficulties of bringing a large fleet into action simultaneously, with an enemy to leeward, the advance being almost in line abreast, is well illustrated by this experience. First, Howe ordered Schomberg to make more sail, probably not realising his ship's capabilities of speed, which seem to have been exceptional, then the *Invincible* grumbled at her for being too far ahead and thus spoiling his shooting: finally Bowyer told Schomberg to keep out of his way!

Schomberg confirmed that, when first sighted on 28th May, the French fleet were in no discernible formation:

> "The enemy seemed at first to come down in a confused manner as if not suspecting it was the British fleet they had in view, and as they neared us they were some hours before they formed in any regular order of battle."

In the main action, Schomberg was one of the captains who were most scrupulous in seeing that (so far as possible) he did not fire into his own side, though he seems to have offended once. His chief opponent was the ship two ahead of the French Admiral. When the battle was nearly over, Howe ordered Schomberg to take station astern of the flagship, to form a reserve in case of attack by less damaged French ships.

Schomberg showed himself active in attacking the beaten enemy: first the three-decked *Républicain*, which one of the French frigates was towing away, and, a little later, ships near his own size.

> "Made sail to take possession of one of the enemy's ships in the E.N.E.", wrote Schomberg confidently. "Two French frigates and a brig attempting to tow off two of their disabled ships; fired at them, and obliged them to sheer off; saw one of their disabled ships get into their line under her spritsail.
>
> "At this time the Admiral made signal to recall distant or chasing ships; the enemy's fleet about 3 miles to leeward of us.

Wore, and stood towards our fleet, informing the Admiral by signal that prizes were not secured; signal was made for us to stay by them; wore again and made sail, but the ships before mentioned had drifted too near their fleet for us to secure them without being exposed to the fire of their line . . . ¼ past 5, firing entirely ceased."

Schomberg's final duty was to take possession of the *Vengeur*, wrecked and sinking as the result of a bloody duel with the *Brunswick*.

VII

The *Invincible*, first ship in Bowyer's division, was knocked about on 29th May.

"At 7", wrote Captain Pakenham, "made the signal to the Admiral that the ship was fit for action but unable from the state of her rigging to keep company. The Admiral made our signal to quit the line."

Next day, Howe sent the frigate *Aquilon* to supply some of Pakenham's needs. She gave help in making masts secure, and later the *Latona* lent two carpenters, and sent across "wads, grease, spikes, oakum, cordage and sails" so that the *Invincible* was well equipped for the serious business on 1st June.

Pakenham was generous in his praise of other ships, particularly the *Royal George*, *Orion* and *Barfleur*, and he was also aware "of the perfect security afforded astern by the discomfiture of the enemy's centre from the *Charlotte* so nobly forcing their line".

Beyond the *Queen Charlotte* was the famous *Brunswick*, and the duel between this ship and the *Vengeur* is one of the epics of the sailing navy. It ranks with the attack by the *Redoutable* on the *Victory* at Trafalgar and the duel between the *Shannon* and *Chesapeake* in the American War of 1812. Both the *Vengeur* and the *Redoutable* sank after action, a rare event with wooden ships of war, however badly they were damaged, since the damage was generally above the water-line, where it could be plugged or stopped. The fight of the *Vengeur* became as legendary in the

25   *A French version of the defence of "Le Vengeur"*

From the painting by Ozanne, 1794

26 *The duel between the "Brunswick" and "Le Vengeur"*
From the painting by Nicholas Pocock, an eye-witness

27 *The Battle, showing "Le Vengeur" sinking*
From the painting, authentic in detail, by Robert Dodd, 1795

28 *Sepia sketch of the scene after the Battle, hitherto unpublished*
From the Journal kept by Edward Baker, of the "Orion"

navy of the French Republic as that of Sir Richard Grenville in the *Revenge* in our own. She did not, however, sink with all hands, as stated in many popular versions of the affair.

These versions were put about as Revolutionary propaganda, on the initiative of Saint-André. Orations were made about the ship in Paris, and an ivory model was ordered to be hung in a public place, in honour of her men. It was said that her ship's company went down shouting "*Vive la République*"—refusing rescue: but an exchange of prisoners which occurred later included her captain! Facts soon punctured a great deal of bombast: but by that time the ship had become a legend, and an exaggerated idea of her prowess was held by Englishmen as well as Frenchmen, Carlyle included. The facts were creditable enough, without any need of embroidery. She fought well.

The log kept by Mr. Stewart, Master of the *Brunswick*, is utterly typical in its matter-of-fact statement of event.

"In breaking the enemy's line," he wrote of the action of 1st June, "got on board the *Vengeur* and engaged side by side, our anchors being hooked."

The time was then about 10 o'clock.

"At ½ past 11," the log continued, "Captain Harvey was dangerously wounded and knocked down; was obliged to go below The engagement was continued, several of the enemy's ships firing at us as they passed. . . . Alongside the *Vengeur* and hotly engaged.

"P.M. Close engaged with the *Vengeur*. The ship on fire at 4 different places. ¼ past 2, the *Vengeur* hauled her colours down, and displayed a Union Jack over her quarter, and hailed for quarter having struck, her masts going soon after and asinking; our mizenmast went overboard. The two ships cleared each other. At ½ past 2, made the signal of inability (i.e. to continue in action), finding ourselves to leeward of the French line and they bearing down on us.

"Called a consultation of officers, the ship being so disabled, could not renew the action. At 3, bore up and began to repair."

At half-past five, the *Culloden* was near the wrecked *Vengeur* and got ready to take her in tow with her boats. Captain Schomberg took the French captain, Jean-François Renaudin, aboard, together with his son. By that time the *Vengeur* was sinking fast:

"... the water then being over her orlop", said the rescuer. "Hoisted out all our boats (except the launch which was shot through) as did the *Alfred* to save the crew; but before we could effect it, she unfortunately went down, and upwards of 300 souls perished. We saved about 130, many of whom desperately wounded and mostly half naked; several died of their wounds on board us afterwards."

Mr. Baker of the *Orion* left the closest account of the end of the *Vengeur*, which was the subject of an accurate painting by Robert Dodd:

"At half past five o'clock, we were witness to the most shocking scene possible. *Le Vengeur* being very much mauled between wind and water in the action filled with water and lay upon her beam ends. Numbers of unfortunate wretches were seen clinging to her side. Soon they were floating in the water and crying for assistance. In a minute's time, she heel'd right over and went to the bottom.

"Numbers were seen floating on the water, of whom the *Rattler* cutter picked up several, but much the greater part of the crew were lost."

Of the dreadful four hours' duel, comparable in noise and horror to one of the infantry battles of World War I, and fought so close that the *Brunswick* could not open her lower deck ports and had to blow them off with her own fire, Barrow adds one or two details. The ship had a large figure-head of the Duke of Brunswick, after whom she had been named. It had a laced hat, which was struck off by a shot. The ship's company, thinking it a degradation that a prince of that house should continue uncovered in face of the enemy, requested Captain Harvey that he would order his servant to lend them his spare cocked hat to repair the loss. Harvey complied, and the carpenter nailed it to the duke's head, where it stayed until after the battle.

One of the sailors wrote to his wife in Devon:

"This dreadful battle happened on a *Sunday*, and if the French have rejected that day out of *their* calender, God Almighty has shown them that he has not left it out of *His*."

Captain John Harvey, who died of his wounds, was brother to the captain of the *Ramillies*, Henry Harvey, whose place was in Hood's first division.

VIII

The *Brunswick*'s division, including as it did the *Valiant*, Captain Pringle, the oldest ship in the fleet, dating from 1759, the *Orion*, Captain Duckworth, and Gardner's flagship, the *Queen*, and going into battle as it did immediately to starboard of the *Queen Charlotte*, won distinction unsurpassed in the British fleet.

There is nothing notable in the log kept by the *Valiant*'s master, Mr. Russel, apart from the fact that the ship provided one of the prize crews, and took on board 173 prisoners, but she was in the thick of it on the first of June, in the later stages in close company with the *Royal Sovereign*, whose station, at the start of the action, was away on the port wing. The partnership of the two ships was an indication of the speed at which a *mêlée* was brought about.

Captain Pringle noted in a letter to Lord Howe that on 29th May he had seen a Frenchman so demoralised that the gunners had left their rammers and sponges in their deserted guns. On 1st June he was so meticulous, at first, in keeping his place in the line, "seeing the enemy dressed to receive us", that he sent an officer aloft to "observe the *Valiant*'s proper place, and found it to be the eleventh ship from the rear". Like one or two others the *Valiant* was not in her normal order of sailing, but she quickly fixed on her opponent, and did well in action, though it was no time before regular order vanished, and Pringle found himself in company with Admiral Graves.

The *Orion*, whose captain, John Duckworth, later (when a Vice-Admiral) won a victory in the West Indies which brought him additional glory, provides, through the journal kept by Mr. Edward Baker, who served in her, details which escaped other eyes. For instance, in the chase of *L'Audacieux* on 25th May, the *Caesar* showed her speed, but by one of those accidents to which she was so prone, she "carried away her jibboom" as she was approaching the French ship.

Mr. Baker noted that on 28th May the French were "continually making signals" and he added that:

> "the whole fleet kept together for the night, and carried as much sail as so stormy a night would permit us, and every man remained at his quarters as we were certain of giving the French battle early the next morning. Frequent hard squalls in the night."

In the more general action on 29th May, Mr. Baker noted the classical French system of gunnery:

> "They pointed their guns very high which did a good deal of execution about the rigging, but we fired chiefly at their hulls, as we thought it best."*

The *Orion* was among the principal sufferers, but, continued Mr. Baker:

> "... at half past 3, having repaired our rigging a little, and seeing very near us one of the French line of battle-ships completely disabled in her rigging and having not a rope standing, we wore ship, and bore down upon her, and running close under her weather quarter, poured a severe fire of great guns and small arms into her, which raked her so effectively, that the Frenchmen ran from their quarters, and the French captain was the only one seen walking the deck, and putting every man to the sword whom he saw fly."

When the *Barfleur* joined the attack, Baker thought the Frenchman must strike, but he did not, and Villaret-Joyeuse bore down to the rescue.

The journal of the Master of the *Orion* gives the order in which the British ships engaged.

* William Parker, a midshipman of the *Orion*, said: "the French called us 'the little black ribband' as we have a black streak painted on our side," adding, "their firing was not very smart, though they contrived to send a red-hot shot into the captain's cabin where I was quartered, which kept rolling about and burning everybody when gallant Mears, our first-lieutenant, took it up in his speaking trumpet, and threw it overboard".

"The *Queen* tacked and led us," wrote Mr. Hunter," as the *Caesar* wore and went to leeward of our line: the *Russell* followed the *Queen*, the *Royal George* followed the *Russell*, the *Invincible* followed the *Royal George*, the *Orion* followed the *Invincible*, when a close and smart cannonading ensued from and at the rear of the enemy. Had our sails and rigging shot away fore and aft. Our mainsail and main topsail quite shot away from the yard, so as only the naked yard appeared. Was obliged to cut away all the wreck to prevent its catching fire."

Mr. Hunter, less laconic than most of his kind, then related how the evening of 29th May and most of next day was spent with repairs, adding:

"Launched ... several empty tubs and butts overboard, as the decks were lumbered with empty casks, to get full ones up for the people. ... Got the masts secured by noon, when it came on a thick fog."

Of the general action he said little, though he managed to cram a good deal of the *Orion*'s affairs into one particular sentence:

"Drove three of the enemy's ships in confusion, who ran to leeward, we being disabled, could not follow, and having no other near to us, but others astern coming up."

Mr. Baker was much more detailed and expansive. "It was", he said:

"a most beautiful sight to see two such large fleets meeting, and keeping up a fire on each other. The fire from the enemy's ships was very smart and fierce before we got close.
"Our fleet did not fire much at first, as we thought the shot would not reach or do any execution. But the French were very smart at firing with long balls, which harassed our ship very much, and an unfortunate shot came in at the starboard side of the main deck and killed George Graham, captain of the 4th Gun and John Leahy belonging to the same gun."

This incident, said Baker, "enraged" and "disheartened" the men. Once ordered to fire in return, all was well. They "frequently gave three cheers at their quarters".

At one time, an opponent who was recognised from 29th May, a "remarkable" ship, engaged the *Orion*, and Baker heard her men cheer as they brought down the *Orion*'s main topmast, "which we returned", he said, "to show we were not disheartened, and we poured our shot into her as she came up."

Mr. Baker even had some praise for the *Gibraltar*, which ship, he said, drew some of the enemy fire. After the action:

> "... the ocean seemed covered with dismasted ships, who still kept their colours flying—two of them from our fleet—*viz*. the *Defence* and *Marlborough*."

The *Orion* fought chivalrously. "Honour", said Mr. Baker, "forbade us to attack ships who were almost in our power." She also had a poet on the lower deck, who produced a ballad which was later sold in the streets of London.

> *Now a health to Captain Duckworth, for he's a valiant man*
> *And all the* Orion's *officers, we'll toast them every one,*
> *Likewise the brave ship's company, that ne'er refuse to stand—*
> *The French to fight was their delight when Duckworth gave command*

> *So now for a conclusion, I'll end my warlike song,*
> *I am a serving fore-mast Jack, to th' Orion I belong:*
> *In praise of all our noble Tars I merrily will sing*
> *Success attend our British Fleet, and long live George the King.*

IX

Next to the *Orion* in the line was the *Queen*. All agreed that her part was outstanding. Her Master, Mr. Mitchell, was killed in action on 29th May, at much the same time that Captain Hutt lost his leg. The ship was fought by Admiral Gardner, with the help of a number of lieutenants. Among them was Samuel James Ballard, who kept a journal and drew plans. Of the later stages of the action of 29th May he said:

> "At 53 minutes past noon, wore ships per signal and renewed the action, passing along the enemy's line within ours. Made four different attempts to break the enemy's line, but could not effect

it. Their rear being so compact left no possibility of sailing ahead of any of their ships, particularly from the shattered state of our ship, who barely steered."

Most of the afternoon the *Queen* was repairing her damage, and at 4.10 Gardner made a signal for the *Venus* to stand by.

"6.10," Lieutenant Ballard continued, "the enemy's fleet wore and stood for us with an intent to cut us off; which they would have done had not some of our own ships very gallantly bore down to our assistance, when they hauled off and wore in a good line."

By that time the *Queen* had twenty-three officers and men killed, and over fifty wounded, including the Captain, two lieutenants and a midshipman; twenty-seven of these wounds were severe.

The *Queen*'s record on 1st June needs to be assessed with allowance for her already damaged condition, and for the fact that her accommodation was full of wounded.

Lieutenant Ballard's description is graphic:

"$\frac{3}{4}$ past 9," he wrote, "the two vans began to engage. Received the fire from several of the enemy's rear ships, going down to bring an opponent to close action, which she easily declined by making sail from us; our ship then being very much disabled in her masts, sails and rigging."

But Gardner was not to be baulked by any retreating Frenchmen. If one would not stand up to his fire, there was always another.

"$\frac{1}{4}$ past 10, brought the next ship to close action, passed through their line and engaged within a cable's length to leeward, sometimes the two ships barely clear of one another", wrote Lieutenant Ballard. "Soon found we had the superiority over our opponent at close fighting, her fire being nearly silenced by $\frac{1}{2}$ past 10; and in much confusion, having suffered us to rake her twice, when her mizenmast, and soon after her main and foremasts went by the board, as did our mainmast nearly at the same time."

Even with further grave damage, and her mainmast gone, the three-decked twenty-five-year-old *Queen* was powerful.

". . . a well directed fire kept up till eleven, when the French ship, being totally dismasted and her fire silenced, called for quarter. Our boats all being shot through, could not take possession of the enemy."

Later in the day, when she was far to leeward of the rest of the British fleet, came the *Queen*'s severest trial, one which was seen with such concern by Lord Howe.

> "Observed eleven sail of the enemy's line and their frigates starting for us", wrote Lieutenant Ballard. "Our fleet so much disabled to windward, no hopes of relief from them. Beat to arms. Swayed a fore studding-sail up for a crossjack to keep the ship from falling down on the enemy. At ½ past 1, they began a heavy fire on us, which was so faithfully returned, occasioned them to pass on, not wishing to have any more fire from a disabled British ship."

"*Beat to arms. . . .*" It was a splendid moment in the history of the ship: and the result was worthy of the defiance. "Lord Howe," continued Lieutenant Ballard, "perceiving our distress, sent the *Pegasus* frigate to our assistance, who took us in tow." To Lieutenant Ballard, as to most of his countrymen, ships were always personal, hence his use, twice, of the word "who" in describing their activities.

Ballard had one more instance of the *Queen*'s splendid self-help to report:

> "½ past 6, having got up a jury mainmast, and after sails [were] set, the *Pegasus* cast us off."

The *Queen* reached home unassisted, though her casualties were greater than any other ship in Howe's fleet, except for the *Brunswick*. Her record was unsurpassed, and it was all the more remarkable in that Gardner was by temperament so nervous that, when the fleet was at sea by night, he was known to rise continually and pace his little stern gallery, making sure that the ship's lights were brightly burning, in case the next astern should come too close.

Writing home after the battle, a seaman of the *Queen* supplied as good a picture of this same Gardner in battle as was ever given.*

* Quoted in *Naval Yarns* by W. H. Long (1899): without precise reference, but an authentic reminiscence.

Private

Sir.

Actuated by a consideration of benefit to the captors, and influenced by that sentiment alone; I would suggest for your concurrence (and if approved, your recommendation of the proposal to your officers and ships company) the Appointment of Mr James Bowen the Master of the Queen Charlotte, to take account of the Stores, and be nominated Agent to the Fleet for negotiating the Sale of the six captured Ships in their purchase by Government, which I conclude will be immediately thought of.

Employed by the Navy Board as he has been for some time, and well acquainted with business of this nature; And having given testimonies of the manly character under my observation which scarce ever fails of being accompanied by the probity suitable to the discharge of such a Trust, I have no scruple in offering this proposition for general acquiescence: No otherwise earnest for the adoption of it,

than as I trust you will see cause to be fully satisfied in the event, by such determination.

My proposition is confined to the idea of a single Agent in the person of Mr Bowen, as I know of sensible disadvantages resulting from the nomination of several candidates for similar appointments.

I have the honor to be Sir

Your most obedient humble servant
Howe

Admiral
Sr Alexr Hood K.B.

---

29 *A letter hitherto unpublished from Lord Howe to Sir Alexander Hood, suggesting James Bowen's appointment as Prize-Agent for the Fleet*

30 (overleaf) *"The British Fleet ... bringing into Spithead the six French Ships captured on the First of June 1794"*
From an engraving by Birnie and Pollard of a painting by T. Luny, 1794

31   *Detail of the Battle: the "Queen Charlotte" in action*
From the painting by P. J. de Loutherbourg

32   *"Le Juste" and "L'América", two of the captured French ships*
in Portsmouth Harbour

From an aquatint by I. Wells, 1794

"I must not omit mentioning the courage of our Admiral," he said. "He seemed quite delighted the whole of the action, and in short you would suppose, could you have seen him, that he was amusing himself at an opera.

"I was quartered on the poop to observe signals, but, owing to the smoke, could not see our bowsprit end, so that in fact I had nothing to do but to stand like a crow to be shot at. There were several poor fellows shot close to me, and if I was daunted or disheartened at that, I had nothing to do but to look at the Admiral—and his very appearance put fresh courage and life into me."

That was on 29th May, when Gardner said that, though he had served at Rodney's great victory of 1782, the fire then was nothing to the speed of the broadsides from the *Queen*: it was, indeed, a subject of general astonishment.

Just before the fleet went into action on 1st June, Gardner called the ship's company together and said that if they fought in the same way a second time, he was sure the French could not stand up to them for half an hour.

One of the men said: "Never fear, Admiral, only lay us close enough." "That I will," said Gardner, "and I'll be bound we'll singe their beards!" There were then such loud cheers that the rest of Gardner's speech could not be heard.

According to the same witness, the *Queen* used 25 tons of powder and 60 tons of shot in firing her 130 broadsides. Her feat stood alone. In less efficient ships it was regarded as fantastic. Incidentally, she was even then a quarter of a century old, and was to be in service for fifty years and to add to her battle honours in the following year, off the coast of France.

X

In the log of the *Ramillies*, the first ship of the rear squadron, there were two entries, one for 29th May and the other for 1st June, which make it clear that her captain regarded signal No. 34 as "permissive"—that is, that captains should break the enemy line if they could, otherwise they were to act as seemed best: At 1.22 was the first entry:

> "No. 34, the Admiral intends to pass through the enemy's line; captains to act as circumstances will admit to engage to windward or to leeward."

The second entry repeats the words almost verbatim. One other entry deserves quotation. The *Ramillies* was used to convey a great many French prisoners, for which she found it hard to find space: on 2nd June her Master wrote:

> "Shook 70 butts (empty) beer and water to make room for the prisoners. . . . Employed taking prisoners out of the captured ships."

Captain Harvey's concern for his brother in the *Brunswick* is shown in the Letter of Proceedings which he sent to Lord Howe after the battle.

> "At 10.55," he wrote "observed the *Brunswick* and one of the enemy's ships to leeward on board each other. Bore down to her assistance and fired our broadside into the French ship's quarter, whose foremast and mainmast soon went by the board."

By 11.15, the *Ramillies* had resumed her earlier station in the line. The ship next to the *Ramillies*, the *Alfred*, ran foul of the *Tremendous* on 29th May, and carried away the starboard stern galleries of Captain Pigott's ship, together with "the cathead and several timbers". The captains blamed each other, but Pigott came off worst. The *Alfred* was not much damaged in action and had no killed. Howe used her after the battle to make rescues from the *Vengeur*, and later to take *Le Juste* in tow.

Alexander Hood's *Royal George* did well both on 29th May and 1st June. She was one of the ships which went to the relief of the stricken *Queen* on 29th May, and her Master noted next day:

> "9. The admiral sent to know if we could stop our leaks. Answered we was ready for action. Engaged refitting. Bore down towards the enemy."

These were fitting remarks for a flagship's Master. Mr. Balmbrough also noted that after the main action sheers were used "for getting up a jury foremast and putting the ship to rights". The frigate *Southampton* was ordered to attend Hood, and she supplied the *Royal George* with spars. "Lost a case of pork," added Mr. Balmbrough, "being shot through—contents 120 pieces." This careful piece of husbandry—entered so as to verify the Purser's victualling accounts—was followed by a note of greater significance. "The wheel very much damaged and tiller ropes shot away the earliest part of the action." The *Caesar* would have made a lot of that.

Sir Alexander Hood never showed up better than on 1st June. He made the *Montagu* change places in the line with the *Royal George*, so that she should be opposed to a 74 and not a larger ship, and his praise for the *Invincible* was generous:

> "It is impossible for me", so he wrote to Howe, "not to give the warmest testimony of the excellent management of the *Invincible* and spirited conduct of Captain Pakenham her commander who kept close astern or rather on the weather quarters of the *Royal George* and sustained the action with true valour."

Hood also had special admiration for the *Queen*, shared by the entire fleet, and for Captain Pringle and the *Valiant*. The *Royal George* had a detachment from the Queen's Royal Regiment serving as marines.* Lieutenant John Smith, of the 2nd Foot, wrote to his mother immediately after the battle to say:

> ". . . after a smart and most decisive action, we have, thank God, gained one of the most splendid victories ever fought at sea."

He hoped that the French would be chased and caught up with before they reached Brest; and he believed there was not much more fight in Villaret-Joyeuse.

> "Our ship and the *Queen*", he added with pride, "are greatly distinguished and much damaged. I am quite untouched."

* Both the Queen's and the Worcestershire Regiment, having several detachments serving with Howe, were allowed a Naval Crown, superscribed "1st June 1794", among their battle honours.

The lieutenant, who showed understanding of sea fighting, added that:

> "The French fought with desperate bravery and great rascality. . . .
> One Frenchman fired into another who had struck. . . . Another
> fired into the *Phaeton* in an equally rascally manner, and killed five
> men: and another would have been blown up by her captain after
> surrendering if the crew had permitted it."

Mr. Smith, in noting that a line-of-battle ship had fired into a frigate, was pointing out that a convention of war had been disregarded. As a rule, frigates were not engaged in a general action by the bigger ships, although if they themselves had the temerity to use their guns, they paid forfeit. Theoretically, a battleship should have been able to blast a frigate out of the water, and this was shown to be true by Saumarez at the Battle of the Nile, when he wrecked the French frigate *La Sérieuse* after she had imprudently tried the effect of her broadside.

The *Phaeton*'s record of the incident bears out Lieutenant Smith except as regards the number of casualties, but shows that she did not submit meekly to such treatment.

> "Passed . . . under a 74-gun ship's stern but did not fire at her,
> she being dismasted, till going a little farther he got his larboard
> guns to bear on us and began to fire on us, which we returned
> for 10 minutes, and during that time we got 2 men killed and 5
> wounded."

The Frenchman's change of gender in the course of a single sentence is significant. The *Phaeton* had one 36-pounder shot through her starboard quarter gallery. This took a man's head off, broke both the thighs of another, and wounded others.

Lieutenant Smith concluded his letter home by saying that the *Royal George* carried 180 prisoners from *Le Juste*, and he repeated, what was perfectly true, that she "had a distinguished share in the business".

There is little to add concerning the remaining three ships of the line. The *Montagu*'s log has not survived, nor has the *Glory*'s. The three-decked *Glory*, though a sluggish sailer, did well in action, and the *Montagu* had three others killed besides her captain. Lieutenant Ross Donnelly reported to Lord Howe that his captain was killed a quarter before ten o'clock on the First of June. He noted that he thought the French had lost ten ships "three of which sunk during the action". At five o'clock he went aboard the *Queen Charlotte* and returned with orders to take station ahead of the Admiral. By that time the *Montagu* had *L'América* in tow. Next day, perhaps not being sure of Donnelly's experience, Howe sent the *Queen Charlotte*'s acting first lieutenant, Thomas Larcom, with a commission to take temporary command of the *Montagu*. Happily Donnelly was not denied promotion by this arrangement. Although two years junior to Larcom, the two men were made commander within a few weeks of the battle. Larcom gained captain's rank in October; Donnelly had to wait another few months, but he lived to reach the list of flag officers before the end of the war.

As for the *Majestic*, the last words of her Master's log add a joyful touch to a great occasion.

> "At noon," wrote Mr. Tracey, under the date 2nd June, "ran under the *Charlotte*'s stern and cheered the Admiral, which was returned, having the *Sans Pareil* in tow."

XI

One of the curiosities of the Glorious First of June was the presence with the British fleet of a hospital-ship, the *Charon*. Nothing was odder than her name, signifying, as it would have done to an age better versed than our own in classical lore, that son of Erebus who, in his boat, conveyed the shades of the dead across the rivers of the lower world. As the *Charon* had a gunner among her officers, she was certainly armed, and nothing in her log indicates that she was used to accommodate wounded after the actions. She did, however, carry not only the surgeons usually found in both ships of the line and frigates, but, in addition, no less a character than Dr. Thomas Trotter, Physician to the Fleet, an authority on scurvy.

There were severe epidemics of various kinds rife in Europe at

the time, and the *Charon*'s main purpose was as an isolation unit
for infectious cases. Disease was found among the crews of the
prizes, *Le Sans-Pareil* having the greatest number, and both
Troubridge and Trotter were shocked at the filth, damp and darkness of her lower deck. Typhus was the worst danger, and there
were one or two cases of smallpox. A lieutenant and two midshipmen from the British fleet succumbed to disease, after having
tended their prisoners.

Howe, who liked Trotter and was deeply respected by the
doctor in return, made much use of the *Charon*. He sent over
seventeen men to her from the *Queen Charlotte*, on the homeward
journey, suspected of fever. Howe seems to have recommended
the continuing use of hospital ships, and they were to be met with
in other fleets during the course of the war.

Perhaps the most remarkable fact in Trotter's account of his
experiences with Howe is his statement of how much even then
the British sailor, in sickness, enjoyed tea, "of all articles of diet,
most relished". After the fleet returned home, Trotter was able
to get the monthly allowance for a 74-gun ship increased from an
experimental "1 lb." to "8 lb.". Cocoa or coffee was a new re-
quisition, 12 lb. a month being provided, and so was "fine soft
sugar" (64 lb.). The supply of barley was increased from 18 lb.
to 32 lb., but invalid sailors seem to have cared little for sago and
rice, and both were reduced in allowance.

Trotter allowed himself one general observation, which would
certainly not have pleased Jean-Bon Saint-André.

> "There is a general impulse among the crew of an English man of
> war to grapple the enemy," he wrote, "or lay him close aboard.
> Frenchmen shudder at the attempt: and whenever it has been
> boldly concerted on our part, they run from their quarters and are
> never to be rallied afterwards. Nor does this courage ever forsake
> them [Britons]: we have seen them cheering their shipmates, and
> answering the shouts of the enemy, under the most dreadful
> wounds, till, from loss of blood, they expired."

7

Lady Mary Rejoices

THE VERY MOMENT he heard of the battle, before any public announcement had been made, King George III wrote a generous letter, in his own hand, to Lady Howe. It ran as follows:

> "*Windsor, June 11th, 1794*
>
> Lady Howe will I trust believe that, next to the Signal advantage to the great cause in which this Country is engaged, nothing can give me more satisfaction than that it has been obtained by the skill and bravery of Earl Howe, and, I sincerely return thanks to the Almighty, without any personal loss to himself. The 1st June must be reckoned as a proud day for him as it will carry down his name to the latest posterity. I will not add more than that I trust now both your mind and that of Lady Mary will be at ease; we must soon hear of his return to Spithead.
>
> GEORGE R."

A few weeks later, Lady Mary Howe, the Admiral's second daughter, was at Portsmouth, in attendance on the Royal Family. The King had come to do honour to the victor, a favour never shown to earlier commanders, and one which was not to be repeated. Lady Mary, wrote a circumstantial letter to her sister Lady Altamont* about the visit, and this, including as it does both an account of the rejoicings after the battle, and action incidents which would otherwise be forgotten, held interest enough to be included by Barrow in his biography of Lord Howe. Its value

---

* By an extraordinary chance, Lady Altamont, Howe's youngest daughter, sailed clean through the French fleet in the fog of 30–31 May, seeing and hearing nothing. She and her husband were travelling in a ship from Lisbon, bound for an Irish port.

today is as a glimpse of pageantry in a gracious century, and as an indication of the regard in which George III was held by his Fleet. It is pleasing that the close association between the Sovereign and the Navy has continued unbroken, and that the sea ceremonies of a less romantic age continue to be colourful.

The Countess Howe went to Portsmouth with her daughter, and the pair dined and spent the evening after their arrival with the Royal family. The ladies "saw them as happy as the general advantage and every consideration of private friendship could make them. . . . The King and Queen, and the older Princesses . . . appeared almost to share our feelings," said Lady Mary.

A visit to the *Queen Charlotte* was arranged for next day. At ten o'clock in the morning, the Royalties went to the Commissioner's house in the Dockyard, where the Countess and her daughter had been desired to attend them. Half an hour later the main party set out for the flagship, the Howe ladies having been sent on ahead to be with the Admiral when he received them.

The King and Queen went to the anchorage in Howe's own barge, which was steered by Sir Andrew Douglas. They were attended by the Lords of the Admiralty in their barge, and by all the Admirals and Captains of the fleet in theirs. They were saluted by the *Queen Charlotte* and other ships as soon as the Royal Standard appeared in sight, and were cheered as they passed.

> "Curtis received the King," said Lady Mary, "and led him immediately upon deck. Our attendance on the Queen and Princesses prevented Mama and I from seeing the first meeting of the King and my glorious father, which I am told was the most affecting thing possible. My father's knees trembled with emotion when he kissed the King's hand, who presented him with a most magnificent sword set with diamonds, and afterwards with a gold chain, to which is to be hung a medal struck for the occasion; which is also given to the other admirals and captains who have contributed to this victory, considered as the greatest ever obtained on the sea."

So partial a judgment was natural in a daughter whose pleasure in the continuing ceremonies was generally shared.

33 *George III presents a diamond-hilted sword to Lord Howe on board the "Queen Charlotte"*

From the painting by H. P. Briggs

Windsor June 11th 1794

Lady Howe will I trust believe that next to the signal
advantage to the great cause in which this Country is
engaged nothing can give me more satisfaction than
that it has been obtained by the Skill and bravery
of Earl Howe, and I sincerely return thanks to the
Allmighty without any personal loss to himself.
The 1st of June must be reckoned as a proud day for
him as it will carry down his Name to the latest
Posterity. I will not add more than that I trust now
both Your mind and that of Lady Mary will be at
ease we must soon hear of his return to Spithead

George R.

34 *The letter from King George III to Lady Howe after the victory*

"My father afterwards kissed the Queen's hand," her letter
continued, "and then his flag was lowered and the royal standard
raised to the main topmast head, and saluted by the whole Fleet."

The visitors then went into Howe's cabin, appearing "happy and
comfortable to the highest degree, giving us a thousand proofs of
the kindest interest".

Dinner was served at three o'clock, and it is to be supposed that
the limited provender of the flagship—Howe had austere tastes—
was supplemented from the shore for the occasion. The meal was
concluded with a toast given by the King, drunk by all guests at
the table: "May her great Admiral long command the *Queen
Charlotte*, and may she long be an example to future Fleets!"

Having complimented the Commander-in-Chief, the King then
honoured the officers and men of the flagship.

"The whole Royal Family walked through the ship's company
drawn up in line," said Lady Mary, "when my Father told the
King aloud 'that their diligence and propriety of conduct, in all
respects, since the victory, was not less commendable than their
resolution and bravery during the action.' Nothing during the
day was more pleasing to me than this walk through these brave
fellows, every one of whom I am certain would attend my Father
to a cannon's mouth, and all of whom have exposed their lives
for him."

The party then left with the same ceremony with which they had
arrived, and were once more saluted by the whole fleet. The
Howe ladies attended the Royal party "to the stairs at the Dock,
and then returned home, perhaps the happiest mortals breathing".

II

Next day, George III held a levée, at which officers of the Navy
were presented. The Admirals were afterwards bidden to dine in
the Royal company, Lady Mary and her mother attending the
Queen. In the evening the party visited the prizes, which were
spruced up as tidily as possible for the occasion.

On the following day there was a launching ceremony, then as now a great occasion, enormous flags flying from staffs on the unrigged upper deck. The ship concerned was the three-decker *Prince of Wales*, and she had her baptism of fire within a year. Afterwards everyone "sailed about" and Captain Stopford gave a dinner on board the *Aquilon*. In the course of the evening the frigate stuck on the Motherbank, the Master having enjoyed himself unduly. Lady Mary's party returned "in boats, having passed a most delightful day, and with the finest weather possible".

Next day being Sunday, the Royal Party went to the dockyard church, where they heard "an admirably fine sermon, which is to be printed, and preached aboard all ships". Our forefathers were connoisseurs of sermons, and it is to be hoped that listening to this one was not one of the penalties of success. This was the day upon which, by the special request of Lord Hugh Seymour, the King dined with Howe's captains. In the evening he walked round the ramparts of Portsmouth, the Queen and the Howe ladies being entertained at the Governor's house.

Monday was fixed as the day for departure, and the ladies were summoned to see the Royal family safely away.

> "To complete all," said Lady Mary, "went by water to South-ampton in the *Aquilon*, and we with them. After seeing them into their carriage, we returned; when the wind, which had been quite favourable to carry them on, shifted exactly round, and brought us home in three hours, the most delightful sail down the South-ampton river in boats I ever went."

The ladies were back at Portsmouth by five o'clock "in time for a second dinner". They were to have left next day, but Lord Howe had had bad news. Captains Hutt of the *Queen* and Harvey of the *Brunswick* had died the day before (30th June), and Howe wished to be at the funeral.

> "Poor Harvey", said Lady Mary, "was his particular friend, and had fought his *Brunswick* in the most heroic manner. His only anxiety after he came into Portsmouth was (his arm having been taken off), that Lord Howe should have been well satisfied with his conduct, and that he had justified the good opinion he had of him. . . . He had received two shots in the arm before he left the deck to have it amputated in consequence of a third."

Lady Mary was told how Henry Harvey of the *Ramillies* had gone to the aid of the *Brunswick*, and how at first it was hoped that John Harvey would survive: "but the hot weather, and a contusion he had in his back, brought on a violent fever." Both Hutt and Harvey had deserved well of their country, and their obsequies were an occasion of proper solemnity.

Lady Mary, being of a cheerful disposition, soon returned to details over which she could rejoice with her sister.

"The King's present", so her letter continued, "has been carried all round the fleet, to every ship's company, and shown to the sailors by an officer, and a paper read to them, written by my dear father, to express that, as Commander-in-Chief, and as he considers this proof of the King's approbation in a great measure obtained by their exertions, he was desirous it should be seen by *all* those who had so much contributed to the victory.

"The sailors have been delighted with this attention, and the sword and declaration have been greeted with three cheers from every ship. Those on board the *Queen Charlotte* all touched it; and the whole Fleet joined in the wish for health of him to wear it. The attachment of the sailors to him is I believe unexampled."

It was so indeed. Although he cared not a rap for popularity, there was seldom a better-liked officer than Howe, and this was proved, three years later, by the way with which, solely by his personal intervention, the first of two general mutinies was subdued. Not even Howe could have settled the more dangerous trouble which occurred later at the Nore, which was the most serious then on record.

Captain Payne of the *Russell* paid Lady Mary much attention, and told her that in the fog of 30th May he had suddenly noticed "a little additional thickness". It was in fact the looming bulk of the *Queen Charlotte*. Payne hailed and asked if all was in order, and how was the admiral?

"The moment it was answered Lord Howe was well, all the men of the *Russell* burst into three cheers."

Lady Mary, in an earlier letter, had apparently told her sister about the *Queen Charlotte*'s men congratulating their Commander-in-Chief after the battle.

"Those who were present", she now added, "tell me nothing was ever equal to it. My father says: 'Poor fellows, I was not prepared for it, and I own it almost got the better of me.' What it must have been to those who saw him take off his hat to return the compliment."

Of the various incidents in other ships, one of the most picturesque concerned the *Marlborough*.

"To this ship", so Lady Mary was told, "two of the enemy were so close that one of the sailors said 'he would visit them on board.' As he was going to leap over, one of his comrades called after him to take a cutlass with him, while he replied saying 'he should find one there.' On being called back, he actually returned with two. . . ."

Barrow believed this incident to be true. Captain Berkeley had told him that when the bowsprit of *L'Impétueux* was over the *Marlborough*'s quarter, a party did indeed board the Frenchman, and found everyone below.

"On board the *Queen* and *Invincible*," said Lady Mary, "the sailors who had their arms taken off in the engagement of the 29 went into the cockpit on the 1st of June, to assist the surgeons and encourage the poor men who were to submit to the same operation, by declaring it was much less painful than it appeared to be, and that they felt no pain from the wounds."

There were even one or two glimpses from the other side. The men of *L'América*, who like those of *L'Impétueux* had run below, assured their captors when their ship was taken that this had been a *ruse de guerre*, and that they had intended to return at the critical moment. Somehow, they indicated, their timing went wrong, but the British agreed that at least the idea was ingenious.

The captain of *Le Northumberland*, François Étienne, actually went so far as to tell Captain Bertie of the *Thunderer* that he was entirely deceived if he thought that the British had gained a victory. No, he said, it was not even worthy of the name of combat. "*Ce n'est qu'une boucherie où vous n'avez montré ni science ni tactique.*" This was an odd commentary on the way in which, over nearly a week, Howe had brought about exactly the result he had aimed at—a general *mêlée*: but to a Frenchman trained in the pre-

Revolutionary school of naval warfare, a *mêlée* was a failure. A victory was won when, by distant cannonading, an enemy was so damaged in his masts and spars that he could neither manœuvre nor chase. By this standard, the French had achieved, even in defeat, a great measure of success, though it was not enough.

> "I think", said Lady Mary of Captain Étienne's remark, "the ferocious courage that could dictate this observation, from a man who was a prisoner to his conqueror, is worthy of admiration, and of a piece with that of the *Jacobin*, who fired her upper guns when her lower deck was under water. . . ."

There was a persistent legend that either the *Queen Charlotte* or, as some said, the *Brunswick*, had sunk *Le Jacobin*, and that she had gone down firing. Although untrue, it is a fact that in several cases even ships' logs, usually the barest and most severe of documents, state that enemy ships were sunk, when it was not so. The *Vengeur* was the solitary case of the kind in the whole series of these operations.

Certainly the French refused to believe that Howe's fleet had suffered nothing more than damage and casualties.

> "The French . . . were so persuaded their fire must sink our ships," said Lady Mary, "that nothing could convince them they had not sunk several. The officers of *L'Impétueux*, prisoners on board our ships, assured Captain Payne they had seen with their own eyes a ship painted red and black, which had particularly troubled them by sticking close to them, go to the bottom, and no declaration of Jack Payne's that he and his *Russell* were *both* above water, could make them credit his assertion. As so many declared themselves eye-witnesses to this fact, Payne and his ship must be considered as *revenants*, for at Portsmouth they or their ghosts certainly are at this moment."

It was natural for the French to believe that they had done more damage than was in fact the case—that loss was not all on one side, and it remains true that the man behind the gun believes himself all-powerful. The most scrupulous retrospect after a battle seldom shakes a man's conviction of the damage he has done.

In cold fact, losses *were* apt to be all on one side in the days of the sailing navies. It was so not only at the First of June, but also at Cape St. Vincent, Camperdown, the Nile, Copenhagen and Trafalgar. Wooden ships being hard to sink, and, when dismasted or partly dismasted, almost immobile, it was not difficult for a victorious side to rescue any ships in danger of capture, when they could not help themselves.

The best examples of survival at the First of June were the *Queen* and the *Brunswick*, both of which were so much damaged that they could have been a comparatively easy prey to an aggressive enemy. But the *Queen*, with the *Venus* standing by, soon got herself ship-shape, and the *Brunswick* was accorded a special paragraph in Howe's original *Gazette* letter.

> "The *Brunswick*", he said, "having lost her mizenmast in the action, and drifted to leeward of the French retreating ships, was obliged to put away large to the northward of them. Not seeing her chased by the enemy in that predicament, I flatter myself she may arrive safely at Plymouth."

Howe's confidence was justified—so much so that it was not to Plymouth that she made her way: she got to Spithead, and would have been ready to defend herself had she been attacked on passage.

III

Lady Mary was a true daughter of Lord Howe in that no details of the actions in the Atlantic failed to engage her attention, from whatever quarter they came.

> "The officers of the *Vengeur*", so she was told, "were carrying prisoners to one of our ships, when theirs went down: and when our people were scarce able to support the sight of our enemies in their horrid situation, the French devils looked on the catastrophe of their countrymen with perfect coolness."

An incident preserved by Lady Mary was also noted elsewhere, and was used as anti-Revolutionary propaganda.

> "The cartridges on board the French ships," she wrote, "taken and used in the Fleet generally, were mostly made of the fine-

painted church music used in the cathedrals, and of the *preuves de noblesse* of the principal families, many hundreds of years old, and illuminated with the genealogical tree. There was a decree of Convention for applying the archives of the nobility to that particular purpose."

"In the matter of nobility", said Lady Mary, there was talk of her father being given a marquisate. The King had wished him to have the Garter at once, but as Pitt had already bespoken the only vacant stall for the Duke of Portland, the honour had to be deferred. Lady Mary thought that Marquis "de la Montagne" would be a pretty title. If bestowed, it would enable her, so she suggested, to be known as Lady Molly Molehill, a name she fancied. "If a French title will not sit well on him," she said, "Marquis of Torbay . . . would completely refute all the insolence of *last* year." In the end, however, Howe declined a step in the peerage.

"I think I have now sent you all my stories," said Lady Mary, "except that Tom Pakenham, having fired away in a very rude style on one of the French men-of-war, and observing they did not answer the compliment in the manner he expected, stopped his fire and desired to know if the ship had struck. On being answered, they had not, he hallooed out, in great rage: 'Then d — n ye, why do you not fire?' "

The letter concluded with some of the toasts which had been given at the dinners to the Fleet. "May the French ever know Howe to be master of the sea!" "The first two words of the Third Psalm" ("*Lord how* are they increased that trouble me . . ."), and another given by the King in person on board the *Aquilon*: "The Admiral, with the Union at the topmast head; he who alone deserves to wear it."

"The common acclamation of the mob at Portsmouth was 'God save the King, and Lord Howe to defend him' ", said Lady Mary. She added: "a good omen. . . . Amongst all the Sovereigns at the figure-heads of the ships, though many were sorely wounded, not *one* crown was either shot or even scratched. This is a fact."

On that cheerful note, the record of festivities and rejoicings ended—monarchy defended, and revolutionaries put down. Howe and his fleet, having enjoyed praise for their success, once more settled to the sober business of defending Britain and her trade, and of preparing to convey her armies across the sea, by which means alone a Continental enemy could be given what Nelson knew as "a *home stroke*". Such sorties were for the future. Some of them were a long way ahead.

Epilogue

HONOURS AND AWARDS IN THE NAVY

LADY MARY HOWE'S talk of gold chains and medals for the admirals of the Glorious First of June introduced a question considerable enough to warrant commentary. It was an aspect of the battle which was of some importance for the future, since a precedent was established which, with modifications, grew into a tradition.

As far back as the days of the Commonwealth and the seventeenth century wars with the Dutch, sea-commanders had been given marks of distinction for services in action, but there had hitherto been no *regular* system of honours and awards either in the Navy or the Army. Special gallantry had, indeed, not gone altogether unrewarded. In 1744, for instance, the Admiralty paid the Mint £100 for a medal and chain for Richard Hornby:

"... Master of the ship *Wrightson and Isabella* ... for his good service in not only defending the said ship, whose crew consisted of five men and three boys, from a French privateer of seventy-five men, but also by firing a shot in at the stern of the said privateer, whereby she blew up and all her crew perished."

Such extraordinary incidents certainly deserved official commendation, but by his recognition of the services of both admirals and captains in the first sea battle of the great war with France, George III was setting in motion a system which was continued and amplified by his successors.

In the eighteenth century, it had been customary to give knighthoods to captains after particularly meritorious actions, and higher awards, including baronetcies and peerages, to admirals after general engagements. There was no other way, except financially, in which gallantry could be recognised, for the hierarchy of decorations and medals which grew up in the nineteenth century did not then exist, and the financial aspect looked after itself, owing to an established system of prize money and prize bounty. Special promotions for services in action affected only lieutenants and those of lower rank, for the rise by seniority of admirals and captains was never disturbed.

Rodney won a peerage for the battle of the Saints in 1782. Samuel Hood, his second-in-command, was given a barony in the Irish establishment, which meant that he became Lord Hood, but did not sit in the House of Lords. Jervis had been given the Order of the Bath the same year for his capture of the *Pégasé*, and Edward Pellew and James Saumarez had been knighted for taking the French *Cléopâtre* and *Réunion* respectively in 1793, the first important single-ship actions of the new war. But although peerages, baronetcies and knighthoods were commoner in the Navy of the eighteenth century than they have been since, it was evident that, in a struggle likely to be of long duration, some other form of reward would need to be established, otherwise titles would become cheap.

A medal was the most practical answer, though the case of Collingwood and others showed that any system of recognition was apt to have defects, and it was argued that awards gave greater cause for discontent than for pleasure. Nevertheless, some such move seemed inevitable. It recognised not merely a commanding officer, but the ship or unit for which he was responsible, and it is not without significance that in the three countries in which a spirit of egalitarianism might be expected to be most evident, Russia, France and the United States, the variety and degree of medals is, and has long been, even more intricate than in monarchical Britain.

If the awards for the Glorious First of June were, by general consent, made on an unsatisfactory system, the matter extended to Lord Howe himself. He got his diamond sword, and a gold medal and chain, but he had to wait three years for the Garter. The matter is explained in a letter, now at Greenwich, which Lady Howe wrote to Lady Altamont.

When he visited Portsmouth, King George III apparently told the Commander-in-Chief, categorically, that he should have the blue ribbon. Soon afterwards, Pitt (always referred to by Lady Howe as "Billy") wrote to Lord Howe to say he understood that the King had "hinted" that a Garter might be given. Pitt said that, while the King's servants "wished to do everything agreeable to his lordship, yet he must say that the Blue Ribbon could at this time be of great advantage to the King's service if it could be disposed of to the Duke of Portland". A marquisate was suggested.

Lord Howe was taken aback, but answered that the King's approbation was his sole ambition, and that "as it was thought that the Ribbon could be disposed of to more advantage, he must entreat it might be given to the Duke". Pitt pressed Howe to take the marquisate instead, but Howe declined. Portland was then Home Secretary, and Pitt depended greatly upon him for influence in the House of Lords. It is unlikely that quiet voices did not tell his Grace who it was that he had made to wait for a star for his coat.

II

When presenting Howe, together with Admirals Graves, Hood, Bowyer, Gardner and Sir Roger Curtis with their gold chains,* the King made it known that medals would follow: large ones for flag-officers, smaller ones for captains. Immediate measures were taken to put these awards in hand, but it was over two years before they were ready for issue.

They were struck at the Mint, and were engraved by Lewis Pingo, from designs made at some earlier date by his father. The Pingos were a family of Italian descent, and were responsible for much fine work during their activity in London. Their large gold medal, two and one-eighth of an inch in diameter, has on the obverse a figure of Victory, standing on the prow of an antique galley, and placing a laurel on Britannia. At Britannia's side is an

---

* Curtis, together with Pringle of the *Valiant*, Henry Harvey of the *Ramillies*, William Parker of the *Audacious*, James Pigott of the *Tremendous* and Thomas Mackenzie of the *Gibraltar* were all included in the flag-promotion by seniority which was dated 3rd July 1794. Captains Gambier of the *Defence* and Seymour of the *Leviathan* were appointed Colonels of Marines.

oval shield, charged with the crosses of the Union Flag. Her right foot rests on a helmet and she holds a spear in her left hand. The reverse carries a wreath of oak and laurel, within which are engraved the name and rank of the recipient, and the date of the action for which it was conferred. Howe's inscription runs:

RICHARD EARL HOWE, ADMIRAL AND COMMANDER-IN-CHIEF ON THE I OF JUNE MDCCXCIV. THE FRENCH FLEET DEFEATED.

When Collingwood received his smaller medal, the inscription was in the same form as that for other captains:

CUTHBERT COLLINGWOOD ESQUIRE, CAPTAIN OF H.M.S. THE BARFLEUR ON THE IST OF JUNE MDCCXCIV. THE FRENCH FLEET DEFEATED.

The captain's medal was one and three-eighths of an inch in diameter and had the same obverse as that for admirals, but in the interest of space the wreath of laurel and oak on the reverse was omitted.

The admirals of the First of June wore their medals attached to gold chains, but similar chains were never again awarded to flag-officers. Later recipients of both large and small medals wore them suspended round the neck from a white ribbon, with dark blue edges. The colour of the ribbon is retained in the existing naval award of the Distinguished Service Cross for officers, and until 1921 was also used for the Conspicuous Gallantry Medal for other ranks. In 1921 the ribbon of the C.G.M. was changed to that of the old and by then obsolete General Service (Navy) Medal of 1793–1840: white with narrow dark blue edges.

It was not until after Trafalgar that gold medals were given posthumously: otherwise Captains Montagu of the *Montagu*, John Harvey of the *Brunswick*, and Hutt of the *Queen* would have received them. Instead, relatives had to be content with a public monument. One particularly unlucky man was Captain Westcott, Caldwell's flag-captain in the *Impregnable*. Both admiral and captain were among those omitted for the distribution, but Westcott

35 *Admiral's Gold Medal and Chain for services at the Glorious First of June designed by Thomas and Lewis Pingo*

Lord How's glorious Victory over the French,

On the 28th and 29th of May, and the 1ft of June, 1794.

YOU brave and warlike heroes that to the feas belong,
It's worth your whole attention to liften to my fong;
The fecond day of May from St. Helen's we fat fail,
Kind Neptune did protect us with a fweet & pleafant gale.

As we cruiz'd along the ocean four prizes there we made,
Our Admiral fent a frigate to conduct them to Spithead,
A fignal then was made for us to fink, burn, and deftroy,
And twenty of thofe merchantmen our fhipping did annoy.

Then we fteer'd our courfe for France, off Breft & Concale
bay,   [at fea;
Where foon we came to underftand the French Fleet were
It was from the Venus Frigate, we this joyful news did hear,
Who was chac'd by the French Fleet but from them the
got clear.

Then How he fpread his lofty wings & after them did fteer
We cruiz'd the feas for feveral days but they did not appear
Until the twenty eighth of May a man fung out aloft,
He faw three lofty men of war, the diftance 3 leagues off.

About three hours after, five & twenty hove in fight,
It proved to be the French Fleet, to us a glorious fight;
To repair unto our quarters we willingly did go,
In defence of our country, to fight the daring foe.

Then our bold & brave Commander from the quarter-deck
he cry'd,
Let every man ftand by his gun to give them a broad-fide;
See your breechings loofe, your tomkins out, your apron
ftrings untie,
And then we fhall be ready to humble down their pride.

The French they being to windward and formed in a line,
Our van fhips did engage them, it's what they did defign;
As all our fleet could not come up Lord How he thus did
fay,
Let bold Pafley and his fquadron engage without delay.

The engagement lafted exceeding hot 'till 9 o'clock at night
But it being fo very dark we could not fee to fight ;
Our Britifh fhips they form'd a line in warlike bold array,
And we gave them a grand falute the twenty ninth of May

Then broadfide for broadfide each other did return,
The rebels fired red hot fhot our Britifh fhips to burn ;
But our Britifh fhot we play'd fo hot, fo furious was our
rage,   [gage.
We broke their line as we defign'd, and gain'd the weather

When we bad them at clofe quarters together clofe we lay,
Till their lofty yards and topmafts came tumbling in the fea
Then this engagement lafted twelve glaffes merrily.
For to maintain the char of the twenty ninth of May.

Next day we could not fee them, it being fo thick a fog,
We repaired all our damages, and toft a cann of grog;
Our Officers and Seamen exerted all their might
To get our fhips in order for to renew the fight.

The thirty firft of May it being the next day,
Twenty feven fail of their line to leeward of us lay ;
And we being but twenty five and night was drawing clofe
Next morning clear we did prepare for them a hearty dofe.

Next day it being Sunday, and on the firft of June, [foon,
Our Captains faid cheer up my lads we fhall be with them
We are fighting for our country, and to maintain a caufe,
Againft thofe fiends who do intend to break our Maker's
laws.

No fooner had he fpoke thefe words the action it begun,
We five of them difmafted by ten in the forenoon ;
Some fay the twelfth of April was glorious to behold
But June the 1ft fhould be engrav'd in characters of gold.

Then their Admiral made a fignal for three fail of the line,
To haul their wind up to us, and fink the bold Orion;
Our main-top-maft being fhot away, we had fo clofe en-
gag'd,
The Culloden and Gibralter took off their fiery rage.

They being fo much difabled they knew not what to think,
When fix of them we captur'd, befides two more did fink,
The reft that we had left for them they would no longer ftay,
But crowded all the fail they could and from us bore away.

His name is Monfieur Villarte, Commander of their fleet,
He faw himfelf difabled and was forced to retreat ;
So now he may go home, the convention may complain,
That brave Lord How reigns fovereign & ruler of the main

Now the action being over, we made the dogs to fly,
Refolv'd we were to conquer them or every one to die ;
So now my boys give loud huzzas, we have the French
dogs beat,
Succefs to all Commanders throughout the Britifh fleet.

The Queen-Charlotte, the Royal-George, the Queen and
the Orion,
All for to lay the rebels low, it was their whole defign ;
The bold Defence and Marlborough, the Invincible alfo,
Before they were difabled, they maue the French to fue.

And as for Admiral Gardner, that man of noble fame,
We'll drink to every one that in memory keeps his name,
Likewife to all our noble tars, like lions, bold and free,
Who nobly fought and glorious beat the daring enemy.

Now a health to Captain Duckworth, for he's a valiant man
And all the Orion's Officers we'll toaft them every one ;
Likewife the brave fhips company, that ne'er refufe to ftand
The French to fight was their delight when Duckworth
gave command.

So now for a conclufion I'll end my warlike Song,
I am a faucy foremaft Jack, to the Orion I belong ;
In the praife of all our noble tars I merrily will fing,
Succefs attend our Britifh fleet, and long live George the
King.

36   *A ballad on the Battle by a Seaman of the "Orion"*

commanded the *Majestic* under Nelson at the Nile, where he fought with distinction. But he was killed in action at his second battle, and as the posthumous rule had not yet come into force, his relatives got nothing. Nelson, in his kindly way, gave the widow one of the Alexander Davison's unofficial medals which were distributed, at Davison's own expense as prize-agent, to every officer and man concerned in the action.

After 1794, matters improved. For their services at the Battle of Cape St. Vincent in 1797, every admiral and captain received the appropriate gold medal. After Camperdown, which was fought in the same year, the only omissions were Captain Williamson of the *Agincourt*, who misconducted himself and was court-martialled, and Burges of the *Ardent*, who was killed.

In the instance of the Nile, Westcott was the sole unlucky captain, Nelson pleading, successfully, for his entire surviving "band of brothers", even including Troubridge, who had missed the actual encounter by getting the *Culloden* stuck on a shoal. Nelson argued that he had saved his ship, and that he had warned the ships following, and thus prevented any further disaster.

No medals were awarded for Copenhagen, Great Britain and Denmark not being formally at war at the time of the action, which was "preventative", but when rewards for Trafalgar came to be considered everyone in command of a ship of the line was honoured, including two lieutenants, Pilford and Stockham, who had fought the *Ajax* and *Thunderer* respectively in the absence of their captains. The lieutenants at the First of June were not so lucky. Donnelly of the *Montagu* who carried responsibility after his captain had been killed, had to be content with promotion. So had Lieutenant Bedford of the *Queen*, though Howe was once heard to say that he would like to have made him a special case. As Admiral Gardner reported, the "almost unequalled zeal and activity in refitting the ship and putting her into a state of defence", when "officers seemed to vie with each other for distinction, and the ship's company in being foremost to execute their officer's commands", did indeed merit some particular consideration.

The great majority of officers and men had to wait until 1848 before the handful of survivors (none of them under sixty except "Baby" McKenzie of the undistinguished *Tremendous*), received the Naval General Service medal designed by William Wyon, with clasp engraved "1 June 1794". Since that time, distribution of Sovereign's awards for services in battle has become at once more general and less tardy.

III

Rewards other than medals in recognition of the First of June were typical of their age. Admirals Graves and Hood became peers on the Irish establishment. Admirals Bowyer, Gardner, Pasley, together with the newly-promoted Curtis, became baronets. Graves, Bowyer and Pasley were also given pensions of £1,000 a year on account of their wounds. First, and sometimes other lieutenants of ships engaged got promotion, and three characters who have contributed so much to this narrative— Bowen and Codrington of the *Queen Charlotte* and Dillon of the *Defence*—all did well, the first two very well indeed.

Bowen was appointed prize-agent for the fleet. This brought him considerable fees, which nobody begrudged. As there was no promotion to be looked for in his own navigation branch of the Service, Howe gave him a commission as Lieutenant, on 4th June—he was confirmed in that rank on the 23rd. His career was afterwards so distinguished that he rose by stages to flag rank, with his portrait at Greenwich Hospital. Bowen was a commander by 1795, and became a post captain in the same year. He was then the proudest man in the Navy, good to serve under, as Dillon was later to discover. He became a Commissioner of the Navy, and had reached the Admirals' list by 1825. As he was 43 years old when he was made lieutenant, his rise was as exceptional as it was deserved.

Codrington, with Howe at his back, also shot upwards. By October 1794 he was commander in charge of the *Comet* fireship. In April 1795 he was made a post captain, and was appointed to the *Babet* frigate. If he had had to wait for a good start, that breakfast at Grafton Street with Lord Howe was certainly the tide in his affairs leading on to fortune. He was a Rear-Admiral and a Knight of the Bath by the end of the war.

As for Dillon, after some successful manipulation of documents to allow for cheating over his age, a matter which was in line with the practice of the age, he became a lieutenant at the age of sixteen. That was good going, even in a century which, in outlook as much as in methods of warfare, differed strikingly from our own.

At the time of the promotion of Lieutenant Larcom, first lieutenant of the *Queen Charlotte*, Howe allowed himself one of his little jokes. Soon after the return of the ship to Portsmouth, he sent for Larcom and said: "Sir, your conduct in the action has been such that it is necessary you should leave this ship." Larcom, who was as brave as his admiral, was thunderstruck. "Good God, my Lord!" he said: "What have I done? Why am I to leave the ship? I have done my duty to the utmost of my power." "Very true, Sir," said Howe: "but leave the ship you must: I have great pleasure in presenting you with this commission as Commander, for your conduct on the late occasion."

As was customary in an age of privilege, rewards were out of scale. Senior officers did handsomely in prize bounty—captains netted £1,400—and the wounded, together with the widows and orphans of the killed, benefited from subscriptions. They came off quite well. Dr. Trotter estimated that gifts from London amounted to between twenty and thirty thousand pounds, and the company of the Theatre Royal, Drury Lane, with the generosity usual in the profession, gave a performance on behalf of the seamen, and raised £1,800 by it. "Reciprocal feelings", said Dr. Trotter, "like an electrical shock, pervaded every corner of the country." ... Lloyds, Trinity House, Edinburgh, and Lord Howe himself, who gave his own big share of prize to the wounded, behaved in a princely way. But for the serving man, lower in the scale, there was not much benefit. Warrant officers received only twenty-five guineas, petty officers received ten, while seamen, marines and soldiers had a paltry two guineas apiece.

163

Dillon told a tale about prize which may serve to round off this chronicle:

"When Mr. Bowen came to the *Defence* my friend John Lee, second captain of the gun from which John West the Swede deserted, refused to receive his share, two guineas.... The honest sailor declared that he would not receive the money offered to him for doing his duty, whilst ten guineas were given to a foreigner for deserting his quarters."

West ranked as a petty officer. Dillon, who was called upon by Bowen, as prize-agent, to explain what had happened in action, thought Lee's was "a noble act, for a man in his class". What became of the two guineas is not recorded, but a little matter like that would not have defeated Bowen.

APPENDIX I

Lord Howe's Letters to the Admiralty

Admiralty Office, June 10, 1794
Sir Roger Curtis, First Captain to Admiral Earl Howe, arrived this evening with a Dispatch from his Lordship to Mr. Stephens, of which the following is a copy:

Queen Charlotte at Sea, June 2, 1794,
Ushant E. Half N. 140 Leagues.

Sir,

Thinking it may not be necessary to make a more particular report of my proceedings with the fleet, for the present information of the Lords Commissioners of the Admiralty, I confine my communications chiefly, in this dispatch, to the occurrences when in presence of the enemy yesterday.

Finding, on my return off Brest on the 19th past, that the French fleet had a few days before put to sea, and receiving, on the same evening, advices from Rear-Admiral Montagu, I deemed it requisite to endeavour to form a junction with the Rear-Admiral as soon as possible, and proceeded immediately for the station on which he meant to wait for the return of the *Venus*.

But having gained very creditable intelligence on the 21st of the same month, whereby I had reason to suppose the French fleet were then but a few leagues farther to the westward, the course steered was altered accordingly.

On the morning of the 28th, the enemy were discovered far to windward, and partial actions were engaged with them that evening and the next day.

The weather-gage having been obtained in the progress of the last-mentioned day, and the fleet being in a situation for bringing the enemy to close action the 1st instant, the ships bore up together for that purpose between seven and eight o'clock in the morning.

The French, their force consisting of twenty-six ships of the line, opposed to his Majesty's fleet of twenty-five (the *Audacious* having parted company with the sternmost ship of the enemy's line, captured in the night of the 28th), waited for the action, and sustained the attack with their customary resolution.

In less than an hour after the close action commenced in the centre, the French Admiral, engaged by the *Queen Charlotte*, crowded off, and was followed by most of the ships of his van in condition to carry sail after him, leaving with us about ten or twelve of his crippled or totally dismasted ships, exclusive of one sunk in the engagement.—The *Queen Charlotte* had then lost her fore-topmast, and the main-topmast fell over the side very soon after.

The greater number of the other ships of the British fleet were at this time so much disabled, or widely separated, and under such circumstances with respect to those ships of the enemy in a state for action, and with which the firing was still continued, that two or three, even of their dismantled ships, attempting to get away under a spritsail singly, or smaller sail raised on the stump of the fore-mast, could not be detained.

Seven remained in our possession, one of which, however, sunk before adequate assistance could be given to her crew, but many were saved.

The *Brunswick* having lost her mizen-mast in the action, and drifted to leeward of the French retreating ships, was obliged to put away large to the northward from them. Not seeing her chased by the enemy, in that predicament I flatter myself she may arrive in safety at Plymouth. All the other twenty-four ships of his Majesty's fleet re-assembled later in the day; and I am preparing to return with them, as soon as the captured ships of the enemy are secured, for Spithead.

The material injury to his Majesty's ships, I understand, is confined principally to their masts and yards, which I conclude will be speedily replaced.

I have not been yet able to collect regular accounts of the killed and wounded in the different ships. Captain Montagu is the only officer of his rank who fell in the action. The numbers of both description, I hope, will prove small, the nature of the service considered; but I have the concern of being obliged to add on the same subject, that Admiral Graves has received a wound in the arm, and that Rear-Admirals Bowyer and Pasley, and Captain Hutt of the *Queen*, have each had a leg taken off; they are, however (I have the satisfaction to hear), in a favourable state under those misfortunes. In the captured ships the numbers of killed and wounded appear to be very considerable.

Though I shall have, on the subject of these different actions with the enemy, distinguished examples hereafter to report, I presume the determined bravery of the several ranks of officers and the ships companies employed under my authority, will have been already sufficiently denoted by the effect of their spirited exertions; and, I trust, I shall be excused postponing the more detailed narrative of the other transactions of the fleet thereon for being communicated at a future opportunity; more especially as my first captain, Sir Roger Curtis, who is charged with this dispatch, will be able to give the farther information the Lords Commissioners of the Admiralty may at this time require. It is incumbent on me, nevertheless, now to add, that I am greatly indebted to him for his councils as well as conduct in every branch of my official duties; and I have similar assistance, in the later occurences, to acknowledge of my second captain, Sir Andrew Douglas.

I am, with great consideration,

Sir,

Your most obedient Servant,

HOWE.

P.S. The names and force of the captured French ships, with the fleet, is transmitted herewith.

List of French ships captured on the 1st Day of June, 1794.

Le Juste	.	.	. 80 Guns.
Sans-Pareil	.	.	. 80
L'América	.	.	. 74
L'Achille	.	.	. 74
Le Northumberland	.	.	. 74
L'Impétueux	.	.	. 74
Vengeur	.	.	. 74, sunk almost immediately upon being taken possession of.

N.B. The ship stated to have been captured on the evening of the 28th of last month, is said by the prisoners to be the *Révolutionnaire* of 120 guns.

Admiralty Office, June 21st, 1794

A Letter, of which the following is a copy, from the Admiral Earl
Howe to Mr. Stephens, supplementary to his Lordship's letter on
the 2nd instant, published in the London Gazette Extraordinary of
the 11th, was received late last night:

In the extract of the Journal herewith enclosed, the proceedings
of the fleet are stated from the time of leaving St. Helen's, on the
2nd of last month, to that of the first discovery of the French fleet
on the 28th of the same. For the farther information of the Lords
Commissioners of the Admiralty, I have now therefore to relate
the subsequent transactions not already communicated in my
dispatch of the 2nd instant, to be delivered by my first captain, Sir
Roger Curtis.

Early in the morning of the 28th, the enemy were discovered
by the advanced frigates, far distant on the weather bow. The
wind then fresh from the S. by W, with a very rough sea.

They came down, for some time, in a loose order, seemingly
unapprised that they had the British fleet in view. After hauling
to the wind when they came nearer, they were some hours before
they could completely form in regular order of battle upon the
starboard tack; the British fleet continuing as before in the order
of sailing.

The time required for the enemy to perfect their disposition,
had facilitated the nearer approach of His Majesty's fleet to them,
and for the separately appointed and detached part of it, commanded by Rear-Admiral Pasley, to be placed more advan-
tageously for make an impression on their rear.

The signals denoting that intention being made, the Rear-
Admiral, near upon the close of day, led his division on with
peculiar firmness, and attacked a three-decked ship (the *Révolutionnaire*), the sternmost in the enemy's line.

Making known soon after that he had a topmast disabled,
assistance was directed to be given to him in that situation. The
quick approach of night only allowed me to observe, that Lord
Hugh Seymour in the *Leviathan*, with equal good judgment
and determined courage, pushed up along-side of a three-decked
French ship, and was supported, as it appeared by Captain
Parker, of the *Audacious*, in the most spirited manner.

168

The darkness which now prevailed did not admit of my making any more accurate observations on the conduct of those ships and others concerned in the same service; but I have since learnt, that the *Leviathan* stretched on farther a-head, for bringing the second ship from the enemy's rear to action, as soon as her former station could be occupied by a succeeding British ship; also, that the three-decked ship in the enemy's rear, as aforesaid, being unsustained by their other ships, struck to the *Audacious*, and that they parted company together soon after.

The two opponent fleets continued on the starboard tack, in a parallel direction, the enemy still to windward the remainder of the night. The British fleet appearing in the morning of the 29th, when in order of battle, to be far enough advanced for the ships in the van to make some farther impression on the enemy's rear, was tacked in succession with that intent.

The enemy wore hereupon from van to rear; and continued edging down in line a-head to engage the van of the British fleet; when arrived at such distance as to be just able to reach our most advanced ships, their headmost ships, as they came successively into the wake of their respective seconds a-head, opened with that distant fire upon the headmost ships of the British van. The signal for passing through their line, made when the fleet tacked before, was then renewed.

It could not be for some time seen, through the fire from the two fleets in the van, to what extent that signal was complied with. But as the smoke at intervals dispersed, it was observed that the *Caesar*, the leading ship of the British van, after being about on the starboard tack, and come a-breast of the *Queen Charlotte*, had not kept to the wind; and that the appointed movement would consequently be liable to fail of the purposed effect.

The *Queen Charlotte* was therefore immediately tacked; and, followed by the *Bellerophon*, her second a-stern (and soon after joined by the *Leviathan*), passed through in action between the fifth and sixth ships in the rear of the enemy's line. She was put about again on the larboard tack forthwith, after the enemy, in preparation for renewing the action, with the advantage of that weathermost situation.

The rest of the British fleet being at this time passing to leeward, and without the sternmost ships mostly of the French line, the enemy wore again to the eastward, in succession, for succouring the disabled ships of their rear; which intention, by reason of the then disunited state of the fleet, and having no more than the two crippled ships, the *Bellerophon* and *Leviathan*, at that time near me, I was unable to obstruct.

The enemy having succeeded in that operation, wore round again, after some distant cannonading of the nearest British ships, occasionally returned, and stood away in order of battle on the larboard tack, followed by the British fleet in the same order (but with the weather-gage retained), as soon as the ships coming forward to close with the *Queen Charlotte* were suitably arranged.

The fleets remained separated some few miles, in view at times on the intermission of a thick fog, which lasted most part of the two next days.

The commander of a fleet, their Lordships know, is unavoidably so confined in his view of the occurrences in time of battle, as to be little capable of rendering personal testimony to the meritorious service of officers who have profited, in a greater extent, by the opportunities to distinguish themselves on such occasions.

To discharge this part of my public duty, reports were called for from the flag-officers of the fleet, for supplying the defects of my observance, under the limited circumstances above mentioned. Those officers, therefore, who have such particular claim to my attention, are the Admirals Graves and Sir Alexander Hood; the Rear-Admirals Bowyer, Gardner, and Pasley; the Captains Lord Hugh Seymour, Pakenham, Berkeley, Gambier, John Harvey, Payne, Parker, Henry Harvey, Pringle, Duckworth, and Elphinstone. Special notice is also due of the Captains Nichols of the *Sovereign*, and Hope of the *Bellerophon*, who became charged with, and well conducted, those ships, when the wounded flag-officers, under whom they respectively served therein, were no longer able to remain at their posts; and the Lieutenants Monkton of the *Marlborough*, and Donnelly of the *Montagu*, in similar situations. These selections, however, should not be construed to the disadvantage of other Commanders, who may have been equally deserving of the approbation of the Lords Commissioners of the Admiralty, although I am not enabled to make a particular statement of their merits.

To the reports from the flag-officers are added those required from the several captains of the fleets; whereby their Lordships will become more particularly acquainted with the meritorious services of the several commanders, and animated intrepidity of their subordinate officers and ships companies; to which the defeat of the enemy, with every advantage of situation and circumstance in their favour, is truly to be ascribed. To the like purpose, I beg my testimony, in behalf of the officers and company of every description in the *Queen Charlotte*, may be accepted.

APPENDIX II

Lord Howe's Fleet

(Order of Sailing)

VAN SQUADRON
First Division

Ship	Captain	Built	Killed	Wounded	Honours
Caesar, 80	Captain A. J. P. Molloy	1793	18	37	
Bellerophon, 74	Rear-Admiral T. Pasley	1786	4	27	Baronet: Gold Medal & Chain
Leviathan, 74	Captain W. J. Hope	1790	10	33	Gold Medal
Russell, 74	Lord Hugh Seymour	1764	8	26	Gold Medal
Marlborough, 74	Captain J. W. Payne; Captain Hon. G. C. Berkeley	1767	29	90	Gold Medal

Second Division

Ship	Captain	Built	Killed	Wounded	Honours
Royal Sovereign, 100	Admiral Thomas Graves; Captain H. Nicholls	1786	14	44	Baron (Irish Peerage) Gold Medal & Chain
Audacious, 74	Capt. W. Parker [28 May only]	1785	4	18	Gold Medal
Defence, 74	Captain J. Gambier	1763	18	39	Gold Medal
Impregnable, 98	Rear Admiral B. Caldwell; Captain G. B. Westcott	1786	7	24	Gold Medal

Ship	Date	Officer			Honours
Tremendous, 74	1784	Captain J. Pigott	3	8	
Culloden, 74	1783	Captain I. Schomberg	2	5	
Invincible, 74	1765	Captain Hon. T. Pakenham	14	31	Gold Medal
Barfleur, 90	1768	Rear-Admiral G. Bowyer	9	25	Baronet: Gold Medal & Chain
		Captain C. Collingwood			Gold Medal (in 1797)
CENTRE SQUADRON **First Division**					
Gibraltar, 80	1780	Captain T. Mackenzie	2	12	
Queen Charlotte, 100	1790	Admiral the Earl Howe			Diamond Sword: Gold Medal & Chain
		Sir Roger Curtis, Kt.	14	29	Baronet: Gold Medal & Chain
		Sir Andrew Douglas, Kt.			Gold Medal
CENTRE SQUADRON **Second Division**					
Brunswick, 74	1790	Captain John Harvey	44	14	Died of Wounds (Monument in Westminster Abbey)
Valiant, 74	1759	Captain T. Pringle	2	9	Gold Medal
Orion, 74	1787	Captain J. T. Duckworth	5	24	Gold Medal
Queen, 98	1769	Rear-Admiral A. Gardner			Baronet: Gold Medal & Chain
		Captain John Hutt	36	67	Died of Wounds (Monument in the Abbey)

REAR SQUADRON

First Division

		Built	Killed	Wounded	Honours
Ramillies, 74	Captain Henry Harvey	1785	2	7	Gold Medal
Alfred, 74	Captain John Bazely	1778	—	8	
Royal George, 100	Admiral Sir Alexander Hood, K.B.	1788			Baron (Irish Peerage) Gold Medal & Chain
	Captain William Domett		20	72	Gold Medal
Montagu, 74	Captain James Montagu	1779	4	13	Killed in Action (Monument in Westminster Abbey)

Second Division

		Built	Killed	Wounded	Honours
Majestic, 74	Captain C. Cotton	1785	3	5	
Glory, 98	Captain J. Elphinstone	1788	13	39	Gold Medal
Thunderer, 74	Captain A. Bertie	1783	—	—	

FRIGATES, ETC.

Latona	Capt. Thornbrough
Venus	Capt. W. Brown
Phaeton	Capt. Bentinck
Southampton	Capt. Hon. R. Forbes
Niger	Capt. Hon. A. K. Legge
Aquilon	Capt. Hon. R. Stopford
Pegasus	Capt. Barlow
Comet, fireship	Commander W. Bradley.
Incendiary, fireship	Commander J. Cooke (Cooke himself was not present)
Ranger, cutter	Lt. I. Cotgrave
Rattler, cutter	Lt. Winne
Charon, hospital ship	Captain Countess.

The French Line of Battle on 1st June

Le Trajan, 74, Captain Dumoutier [Neilly's Squadron]
L'Éole, 74, Captain Bertrand Keranguen
L'América, 74, Captain Louis L'Héritier [*Prize*]
Le Téméraire, 74, Captain Morel [Neilly's Squadron]
Le Terrible, 110 { Rear Admiral François-Joseph Bouvet [Second in Command]
Captain Julian Le Ray
L'Impétueux, 74, Captain Douville [*Prize*]
Le Mucius, 74, Captain Larréguy.
Le Tourville, 74, Captain Langlois
Le Gasparin, 74, Captain Tardy
La Convention, 74, Captain Joseph Allary
Le Trente-et-Un-Mai, 74, Captain Honoré Ganteaume [Cancale or St. Malo Squadron]
Le Tyrannicide, 74, Captain Dordelin
Le Juste, 80, Captain Blavet [*Prize*]
Le Montagne, 120 { Rear Admiral Louis-Thomas Villaret-Joyeuse [Commander-in-Chief]
M. Jean-Bon Saint-André [Naval Commissioner]
Captain Bazire
Le Jacobin, 80, Captain Gassin
L'Achille, 74, Captain de la Villegris [*Prize*]
Le Vengeur Du Peuple, 74, Captain Jean-François Renaudin [*Sunk*]
La Patriote, 74, Captain Lucadou [Neilly's Squadron]
Le Northumberland, 74, Captain François Étienne [*Prize*]
L'Entreprenante, 74, Captain le Francq
Le Jemmapes, 74, Captain Desmartis
Le Neptune, 74, Captain Tiphaine
Le Pelletier, 74, Captain Berrade
Le Républicain, 110 { Rear Admiral Joseph-Marie Neilly
Captain Pierre-Jacques Longer
Le Sans-Pareil, 80, Captain Jean-François Courand [*Prize*]
Le Scipion, 80, Captain Huguet

APPENDIX IV

Sources and Acknowledgments

Chapter

1   Sir John Barrow, *The Life of Richard Earl Howe*, 1838. A British Museum copy (C. 45 d. 27) has annotations by Lady Bouchier

2   Lady Bouchier, *Memoir of the Life of Admiral Sir Edward Codrington*, 1875. A British Museum copy (C. 45 f. 12) has been annotated by the author from Codrington's own notes

3   E. P. Brenton, *The Naval History of Great Britain*, Vol. I, 1837. This edition contains additional notes

    E. Chevalier, *Histoire de la Marine Française*, 1886

    L. Levy-Scheider, *Le Conventionnel Jean-Bon Saint-André*, 2 vols, 1901

    A. T. Mahan, *The Influence of Sea Power upon the French Revolution and Empire*

4   Sir William Dillon, *A Narrative of My Professional Adventures, 1790–1802* [Ed. Michael Lewis, *Navy Records Society*, Vol. I, 1953]

5   *The Private Correspondence of Admiral Lord Collingwood* [Ed. Edward Hughes, *Navy Records Society*, 1957]

6   Edward Baker, *Journal* (Greenwich MS.)

    Matthew Flinders, *Journal* (Greenwich MS. 60/017)

    William James, *The Naval History of Great Britain*, 1886

    Logs of the Great Sea Fights [Ed. T. Sturges Jackson, *Navy Records Society*, Vol. I, 1899]

    The Original Dispatches Commemorating the Principal Victories Obtained by the British Navy over the Fleets of France and her Allies in the Course of the Revolutionary Wars, 1794–1866 (B.M. Add. MS. 23, 207 presented to the Museum by the Admiralty)

    Thomas Trotter, *Medicina Nautica*, 2 vols, 1797–99

7   Greenwich MS. 58/102 (Howe/2, Howe/116). Barrow

8   Sir John Craig, *The Mint*, 1953

    Mariner's Mirror, Vol. 23, No. 3 (1937) and Vol. 37, No. 4 (1951) These volumes contain valuable articles by Commander W. B. Rowbotham, R.N., on the subject of earlier awards to the Navy

Index

Index

The numerals in **heavy type** denote the *figure numbers* of the illustrations

179